MATH TREK 2

A Mathematical Space Odyssey

IVARS PETERSON

and

NANCY HENDERSON

New York • Chichester • Weinheim • Brisbane • Singapore • Toronto

This book is printed on acid-free paper. ∞

Published by John Wiley & Sons, Inc.
Published simultaneously in Canada
Design and production by Navta Associates, Inc.

Credits
Page 3: © 1999 European Southern Observatory; Page 7 (left): Phyllotaxis spiral © Michael Trott, Wolfram Research; Pages 5, 7, 9, 34: Photographs by I. Peterson; Pages 21 (bottom), 48, 52: Courtesy of Stan Wagon, Macalester College; Page 22: © Cordon Art B. V.; Page 49: Photograph © Greg Helgeson; Pages 83, 84: Courtesy of Tom Banchoff, Brown University.

This publication is designed to provide accurate and authoritative information in regard to the subject matter covered. It is sold with the understanding that the publisher is not engaged in rendering professional services. If professional advice or other expert assistance is required, the services of a competent professional person should be sought.

ISBN: 0-471-31571-0

Printed in the United States of America
10 9 8 7 6 5 4 3 2 1

To our sons,
Eric and Kenneth

Contents..................

Preface..

Mathematics can take you places where you have never been before. When you explore a mathematical universe you observe amazing patterns, solve intriguing puzzles, and stretch your imagination into the far reaches of the mind. Samples of the phenomenal shapes and patterns you encounter in mathematics also show up in daily life right here on Earth! Look at a daisy, kick a soccer ball, or untangle a string, and you are in touch with the exotic wonders of mathematics.

You don't have to be a professional to enjoy mathematical patterns and puzzles. Solving mathematical puzzles can be a passion, just as playing baseball, making music, or riding horses can be a passion for those who enjoy it. There is fun and challenge at every level, so set your mind on the launching pad and be ready for a wild trek into the mathematical universe.

A Consequential Countdown

"**C**lean up your room right this minute," your mother says. "You may not go out until all that stuff is put away."

You flop onto your bed, dreading the prospect of having to sort through all those cards and papers and books and games and socks and shoes and . . .

WOLK-STANLEY 2000

. . . just thinking about it makes you feel tired. You are starting to feel sleepy . . . very sleepy . . . and your eyes close. . . .

Suddenly you open your eyes and realize you must have dozed off. Gazing up at the flat, dull ceiling of your bedroom, you remember the mess you were supposed to clean up. Now it's dark outside. Your curtains are still open, and through the window you see a sky full of stars.

You hear a noise that sounds like a distant motor. Soon it grows louder than an air conditioner, then louder than a lawn mower, then even louder than a huge truck. Your bed starts to move, as if powered by its own engine. The mattress folds up, propping you in a sitting position.

Your eyes search the room. Where is all your stuff? Who cleaned up the mess? Your desk is now covered with high-tech displays and a keyboard instead of papers and books. Mounted high on the wall in front of you is a huge computer screen.

"PREPARE FOR TAKEOFF!" blares a voice from your bedroom radio. The number "55" flashes on the screen, and the voice roars, "FIFTY-FIVE!"

A second later, the voice from your radio shrieks, "THIRTY-FOUR!" as the flashing number on the screen changes to "34."

"TWENTY-ONE!"

"THIRTEEN!" If this is a countdown, you wonder, why does it skip so many numbers?

"EIGHT!"

"FIVE!"

"THREE!" You shiver with trepidation as an automatic seat belt locks over you.

"TWO!" Your heart pounds faster and faster.

"ONE!" You shut your eyes and clench your fists.

"ONE!" One again? Is the countdown stuck?

EXPLOSION! You feel the whole room shudder as it takes off.

Your body feels pressed down into the seat, as if there is a tremendous amount of gravity. Looking out the window, you realize that you really are heading into space.

After a couple of minutes, the motor quiets down. Your body starts to feel eerily light. Unbuckling the seat belt, you find that you can push off from your chair and float over to the window.

Clutching the windowsill, you can make out Earth's blue oceans and brown and green continents as the planet grows smaller and smaller. Then you gaze into space and see thousands of stars and dozens of spiral-shaped galaxies.

Stars and spiral galaxy.

Why are there so many spirals? Why did the countdown skip numbers and repeat the number "1"? What in the cosmos is going on here?

[Answers follow.]

A Special Sequence

Remember the puzzling countdown 55, 34, 21, 13, 8, 5, 3, 2, 1, 1?

Look at it in reverse order: 1, 1, 2, 3, 5, 8, 13, 21, 34, 55. Do you see a pattern? Can you predict what number would come next?

The numbers belong to a famous sequence named for the Italian mathematician Fibonacci, who lived more than seven hundred years ago. Each consecutive number is the sum of the two numbers that precede it. Thus, 1 + 1 = 2, 1 + 2 = 3, 2 + 3 = 5, 3 + 5 = 8, and so on.

The ninth number of the **Fibonacci sequence** is 34 and the tenth is 55, so the eleventh is 89. What is the twelfth Fibonacci number? What is the sixteenth?

[Answers on p. 103]

TRY it

Here are some additional number sequences. See if you can fill in the missing numbers and figure out the rules for making each sequence.

• • • • • • • • • •

1, 3, 4, 7, 11, 18, 29, 47, ____, 123, . . .

3, 6, 12, 24, 48, ____, 192, 384, . . .

1, 3, 6, 10, 15, 21, 28, 36, ____, 55, 66, 78, . . .

1, 4, 9, 16, ____, 36, 49, 64, 81, 100, . . .

[Answers on p. 103]

Number sequences have intrigued mathematicians for centuries. The first example given above is called the **Lucas sequence,** honoring the nineteenth-century French mathematician Édouard Lucas, who studied the Fibonacci sequence. Lucas worked out what would happen if you started with any two whole numbers, then followed the Fibonacci rule. He discovered many interesting new sequences and number patterns.

Neil Sloane, a mathematician at Bell Labs, has been collecting number sequences ever since he was a student at Cornell University in the 1960s. He describes nearly six thousand examples in his book the *Encyclopedia of Integer Sequences*. Mathematicians and other researchers use his book as a reference for counting or tabulating things that involve number sequences, from the number of atoms in various molecules to different types of knots.

• • •

Nature's Numbers

If you have ever looked for a four-leaf clover, you know that they are very hard to find because nearly every clover has exactly three leaves.

If you study the petals on different flowers, you'll discover that the most common number of petals is five. Buttercups, geraniums, pansies, primroses, rhododendrons, tomato blossoms, and many other flowers have five petals.

You will also find flowers that have eight petals (e.g., delphiniums), thirteen petals (ragwort), and twenty-one petals (black-eyed Susans). Fibonacci numbers—3, 5, 8, 13, and 21—crop up surprisingly often in plants, from the clustering of petals on a flower to the arrangement of leaves on a stem.

Flowers often have three, five, or eight petals.

Examine flower petals to find Fibonacci numbers.

YOU WILL NEED
- books or catalogs with pictures of flowers, or actual flowers you can observe
- pencil and paper

WHAT TO DO

1. Count the number of petals on each flower and record the totals. Check several examples of the same species if possible to see if each flower of the same type has exactly the same number of petals. If they differ, record the most common number of petals or the average number.

2. Check how many of your totals are Fibonacci numbers. Can you find any flowers for which the number of petals is not a Fibonacci number?

[Answer on page 103.]

Spiral Arms

It's not unusual to find spirals in nature—in the shapes of nautilus shells, among some kinds of spiderwebs, and in the arms of many galaxies. Plants often feature spirals, too.

Pineapples have rows of scales, which spiral around both clockwise and counterclockwise.

Pineapples and pine cones have rows of diamond-shaped markings, or scales, which spiral around both clockwise and counterclockwise. If you count the number of scales in one of these spirals, you are likely to find 8, 13, or 21.

In the head of a sunflower, the tiny florets that turn into seeds are typically arranged in two intersecting families of spirals, one winding clockwise and the other winding counterclockwise. Count the number of florets along a spiral and you are likely to find 34, 55, 89, or 144—all Fibonacci numbers, of course.

The head of a sunflower displays two intersecting families of spirals, as shown in the diagram of a typical seed arrangement.

The Golden Ratio

Why do Fibonacci numbers come up so often in the natural world?

The answer has to do with an amazing link between the Fibonacci sequence and a remarkable number known as the **golden ratio.**

Below is a special rectangle of length A and width B. The length of side A divided by side B is about 1.618. If you tried to write out the exact decimal value, you would find that the string of digits never comes to an end. The number 1.618 . . . is called the golden ratio. Any rectangle with sides that correspond to the golden ratio is known as a **golden rectangle.**

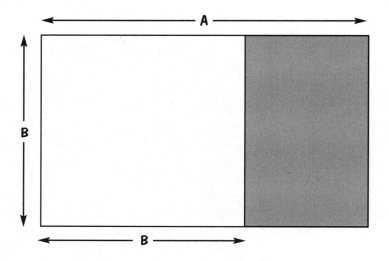

Cutting off a square from a golden rectangle leaves a new rectangle
(shaded) with sides that also correspond to the golden ratio.

If you cut off a square (B x B) from the original rectangle, that leaves a new, smaller rectangle. The length of this new rectangle divided by its width is also 1.618 . . . ! If you cut off a square from this smaller rectangle, it would leave another rectangle with the sides in the same ratio, 1.618 . . . ; you can continue this process forever, creating smaller and smaller rectangles and squares, with the same result each time.

When you draw a curve connecting the corners of these nested rectangles, you form a spiral! That's the same sort of spiral that you find in many seashells, snail shells, spiderwebs, and even stars clustered in galaxies.

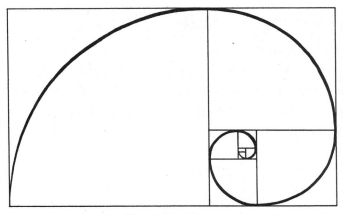

The diagonally opposite corners of a set of squares nested within a golden rectangle can be joined by curves to create a spiral.

Ancient civilizations believed the golden ratio to have divine and mystical properties. For example, in ancient Greece, the Parthenon, completed in 438 B.C., was constructed so its front face forms a golden rectangle.

It turns out that the ratio of any consecutive pair of numbers in the Fibonacci sequence is approximately the golden ratio. For instance, 3/2 is 1.5, 5/3 is 1.666 . . . , 8/5 is 1.6, and so on. As the numbers in the sequence get larger, the ratios of consecutive numbers get closer to the golden ratio.

The Greek temple known as the Parthenon sits atop a hill in the city of Athens. The building's width to height has the same ratio as the golden rectangle.

The golden ratio appears in certain rectangles, and it also appears in some regular geometric shapes, such as the pentagon (five-sided figure) and the five-pointed star. Try to calculate the golden ratio from measurements of a golden rectangle and a regular pentagon.

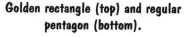

YOU WILL NEED

- sheet of paper
- pencil
- ruler
- calculator

Golden rectangle (top) and regular pentagon (bottom).

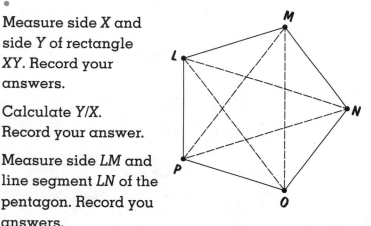

WHAT TO DO

1. Measure side *X* and side *Y* of rectangle *XY*. Record your answers.

2. Calculate *Y/X*. Record your answer.

3. Measure side *LM* and line segment *LN* of the pentagon. Record you answers.

4. Calculate *LN/LM*. Record your answer.

5. Compare your answer in step 2 with your answer in step 4.

6. Can you find other pairs of measurements in the pentagon diagram that correspond to the golden ratio?

[Answers on page 103.]

FIBONACCI AND HIS RABBITS

Leonardo of Pisa, who lived from about 1170 to about 1240, was the greatest European mathematician of the Middle Ages. He was also called Fibonacci, which means "son of Bonaccio." Although he was born in Pisa, Italy, Fibonacci received much of his early mathematical training from Muslim tutors in Algeria, where his father was an official in an Italian trading business.

Fibonacci's teachers introduced him to the Arab and Hindu numbering system we use today. He recognized the system's many advantages over the clumsy Roman numerals used in Italy at the time. (Try multiplying XLVIII by CCXI!)

In a math handbook he wrote for merchants, Fibonacci explained the advantages of Hindu-Arabic notation. Titled *Liber abaci* (*Book of the Abacus*), the book helped introduce the decimal numbering system to Europe.

The number sequence named after Fibonacci comes from an arithmetic problem in his book. Suppose a pair of rabbits is placed in an enclosure to breed. After two months they breed one female and one male rabbit and another pair each month afterward. Each new pair of rabbits also breeds a pair of rabbits starting after two months. So after four months there are three pairs of rabbits and after five months there are five pairs (see illustration on page 12). If you keep on counting the total number of rabbit pairs each month, you get the numbers of the Fibonacci sequence.

In Fibonacci's rabbit problem, a pair of newborn rabbits waits two months before producing offspring, so only one pair of rabbits is present the first and second months (first two columns). It produces offspring in the third month, so now a total of two pairs of rabbits are present (third column). In the fourth month, the original pair produces another pair, but the other pair isn't ready to produce offspring yet, giving a total of three pairs of rabbits (fourth column).

1   2   3   4   5

Planet of the Shapes

All is silent and peaceful as your bedroom-turned-spacecraft sails smoothly through space. Out the window you see bright stars and spiral galaxies, and you see the same view on your computer screen as you move along.

Suddenly a brilliant green dot appears on the screen. You reach for the computer mouse on your desk and click on the dot. The glistening green dot grows into a multicolored, sparkling sphere. You click on the sphere again and it grows larger. Now it looks like a bright, multicolored soccer ball! Its surface is covered with a pattern of five-sided and six-sided patches, which are **pentagons** (five-sided) and **hexagons** (six-sided).

You click on one of the pentagons, and it expands to fill the entire screen. Now you see that it is made up of a curious pattern of diamond shapes. Some of the diamonds are fat; others are skinny.

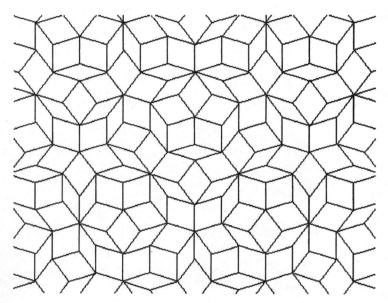

This curious pattern is made from just two types of tiles: fat and skinny diamonds.

All at once a loud roar fills the room, and you feel your stomach rising, as if you were descending in an elevator. Then suddenly it's quiet.

You stand up, walk over to the window, and stare out in disbelief. You seem to have landed on a very weird planet. There are no rocks and no hills. You see no Martian desert and no mysterious jungle. The scene outside your window looks more like the floor of a giant's bathroom than a natural landscape. The flat "ground" is covered with diamond-shaped tiles, some fat and some skinny, arranged in the same curious pattern that appeared on your screen.

You step outside and walk along on the tiled floor until you come to a sign and a map:

Welcome to Penrose Plaza

Using the map as a guide, you make your way toward Checkerboard City, stepping from one fat or skinny diamond tile to the next. Before long, you come to a vast checkerboard. Turning to the right, you head in the direction of Triangle Terrace. Sure enough, there you see a terrace paved with triangles. Then you proceed through Octagon Square and Honeycomb Haven.

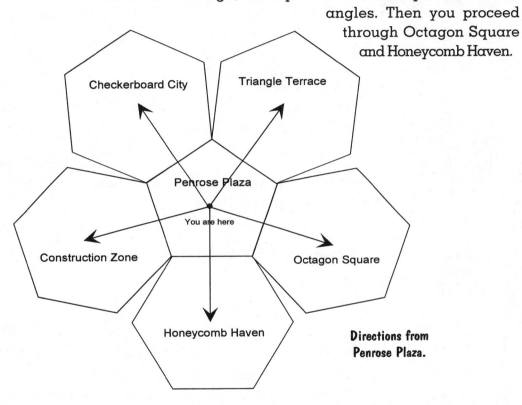

Checkerboard City

Triangle Terrace

Penrose Plaza

You are here

Construction Zone

Octagon Square

Honeycomb Haven

Directions from Penrose Plaza.

Ambling on, you at last arrive at the Construction Zone. It's a total mess! The floor is bare and black, and tiles of different shapes and colors are scattered all around: hexagons, squares, rectangles, and diamonds.

Just for fun, you decide to play around with the pieces. Using only the squares, you find that you can easily cover the ground, leaving no bare spots. You try covering the ground with triangles. Then you cover it with hexagons. No bare spots!

Instead of using just one type of piece, you try to cover the ground using a mixture of squares, triangles, and hexagons. Can you fit the shapes into a pattern without leaving any gaps?

[Answers follow.]

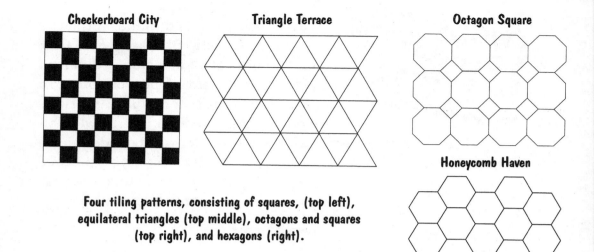

Checkerboard City   **Triangle Terrace**   **Octagon Square**

Honeycomb Haven

Four tiling patterns, consisting of squares, (top left),
equilateral triangles (top middle), octagons and squares
(top right), and hexagons (right).

TRY it

Cut out paper squares, triangles, and hexagons, then use
them to create tiling patterns.

YOU WILL NEED

- lots of paper tiles! (Make at least five copies of p. 17.)
- scissors
- flat surface

WHAT TO DO

1. Cut out the shapes on the pages you have copied.

2. Try fitting together squares and triangles so they cover
   your flat surface completely, without leaving any gaps
   and without overlapping. Can you create a pattern that
   repeats itself?

3. This time, try covering your surface with a repeating pattern of triangles and hexagons. Is there more than one
   possibility?

4. Try using all three shapes—triangles, squares, and
   hexagons—to create a repeating pattern that covers the
   surface.

[Answers on pp. 103–104]

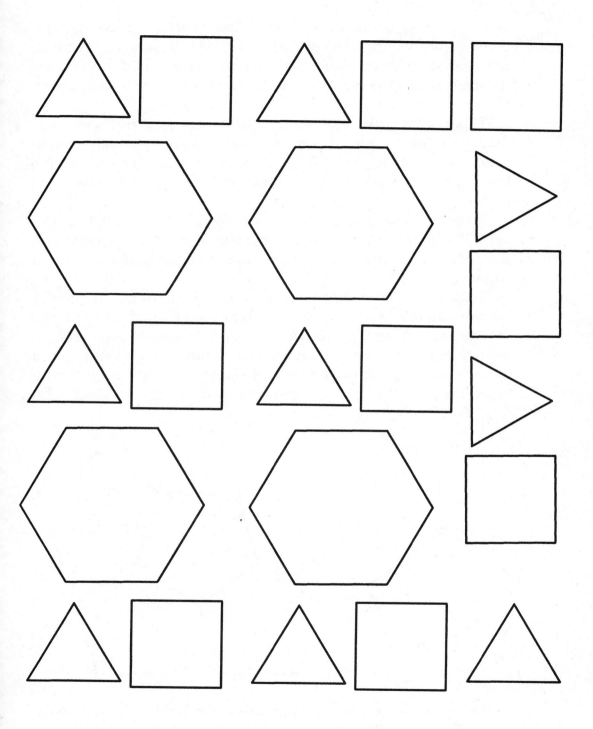

Paving the Plane

From the tiles you see on bathroom floors to the intricate designs found on Native American pottery and Middle Eastern rugs, repeating geometric patterns have been inspiring artists all over the world for thousands of years. Such patterns also fascinate mathematicians.

Tiling is the process of fitting together flat geometric shapes so that pieces cover an infinitely large flat surface—what mathematicians call a **plane**—without overlapping one another or leaving any gaps. The result is a kind of jigsaw puzzle that stretches off to infinity.

No one knows how many different combinations of tile shapes can fill a plane. There are an enormous number of possibilities, but only the simplest ones have been completely identified and cataloged.

Suppose you start with straight-sided figures called **polygons**. A **regular polygon** has all its sides the same length and all its angles the same size. A square is an example of a four-sided regular polygon with 90-degree angles, and an equilateral triangle is an example of a three-sided regular polygon with 60-degree angles. A regular pentagon has five sides, and each angle between its adjacent sides is 108 degrees.

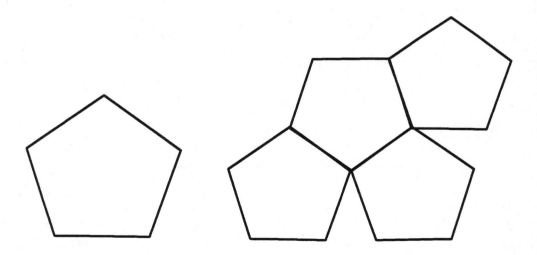

A regular pentagon has five sides of equal length and five equal interior angles (left). Tiles of this shape can't be fitted together without creating overlap or leaving gaps (right).

Checkerboard City, Triangle Terrace, and Honeycomb Haven are examples of how equilateral triangles, squares, and regular hexagons can fit together to cover a flat surface. If you tried to use regular pentagons, however, you would end up with gaps in your pattern. In fact, there are only three ways to tile a plane with a single type of regular polygon.

The next step is to consider patterns in which two or more regular polygons are fitted together corner to corner, so that the same tiles, in the same order, surround each corner, or **vertex**. There are exactly eight ways to do this using various combinations of triangles, squares, hexagons, octagons, and dodecagons (twelve-sided polygons). Any of these eight combinations would make a nice floor tiling.

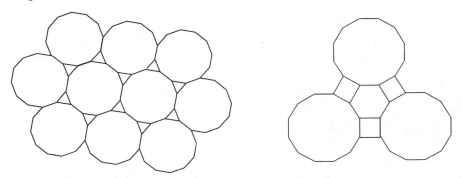

Two of the eight ways to fit together different types of regular polygons involve dodecagons. One tiling pattern requires dodecagons and triangles (left) and the other dodecagons, squares, and hexagons (right).

Change the tiling rules a little bit to allow other shapes and combinations, and you readily end up with an infinite number of possibilities.

The polygons don't have to be regular, for instance. Lifting the restriction that all sides have to be equal in length and all angles between sides must have the same measure means that you can cover a surface with certain types of pentagons—even though you can't do it with regular pentagons.

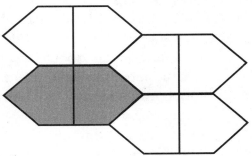

Dividing an elongated hexagon in half produces two pentagons, as seen in the shaded section. Unlike regular pentagons, these pentagons can be used to tile the plane.

HONEYCOMBS

When honeybees mold wax to construct honeycombs for storing honey, they create a grid of hexagonal cells. Mathematicians have now proved that a hexagonal grid represents the best way to divide a surface into equal areas with the smallest total **perimeter** (length of the outside edge). When it comes to using wax, bees certainly know how to economize!

Sorting Patterns

To study different tilings, mathematicians sort them into different categories.

One way to classify tiling patterns is by their type of **symmetry.** Symmetry often involves balance, harmony, and proportion. A

checkerboard design is symmetric, but random splashes of paint are not. Many natural objects are symmetric, from flowers and fish to crystals and leaves.

There are many different types of symmetry. A design has mirror, or reflectional, symmetry if it can be folded along a line so that all the points on one side of the fold exactly coincide with corresponding points on the other side of the fold.

A design has rota-

This tiling pattern has mirror symmetry. The left half is a mirror image of the right half, and the top half is a mirror image of the bottom half.

tional symmetry if it can be traced and rotated less than a complete cycle about a point so that the tracing matches the original design. A pentagon and a starfish both have fivefold rotational symmetry, because you can turn either object one-fifth of the way around without changing its appearance. An equilateral triangle has threefold symmetry.

The pattern inside the square has threefold rotational symmetry. Turning the pattern 120 degrees (one-third of the way around) matches the original design.

Many symmetric tilings are also **periodic,** which means that a basic pattern of one or more tiles is repeated throughout the entire tiling design. Mathematicians have found that there are seventeen different types of symmetry among tiling patterns that repeat themselves. These periodic patterns appear in artwork all over the world, from the intricate tiles on Islamic buildings to the geometric patterns on African textiles.

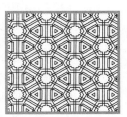

These examples represent four of the seventeen different types of symmetry possible in a repeating wallpaper pattern.

Special Tiles

The design on Penrose Plaza, composed of fat and skinny diamonds, is an example of a Penrose tiling. It is named after the mathematical physicist Roger Penrose, who, in the 1970s, found a way to assemble two related shapes, which he called "kites" and "darts," into patterns that cover a flat surface without leaving any gaps.

What makes both the kite-and-dart pattern and the diamond pattern special is that the tilings are not periodic. They do not repeat themselves at regular intervals, so the patterns are irregular. Interestingly, the tiles in both types of patterns have dimensions that are related to the golden ratio (see Trek 1). For example, the distance from the sharp tip to the blunt end of a kite tile equals the distance from the notch to the sharp tip of a dart tile times the golden ratio.

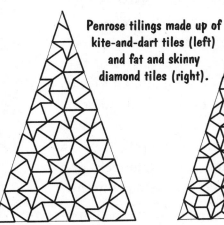

Penrose tilings made up of kite-and-dart tiles (left) and fat and skinny diamond tiles (right).

Penrose was just playing around when he first put together his nonperiodic tiling. Several years later, scientists discovered a group of strange materials, called "quasicrystals," made up of metal atoms arranged in an unexpected pattern. Penrose's tiling patterns gave scientists hints on how it might be possible to position atoms to create an orderly but nonrepeating structure.

TILINGS THAT COME TO LIFE

Tilings don't have to be limited to polygons. Many of the drawings by M. C. Escher, a Dutch artist who lived from 1898 to 1972, contain fascinating tiling patterns with tiles in the shape of birds, fish, reptiles, or other living things.

As a young boy, Escher felt an irresistible urge to fill space neatly with small pieces. Drawing was his favorite subject in school, and after graduating, he became a graphic artist. At age twenty-four, he visited Spain and discovered the intricate mosaic designs in the Alhambra, a thirteenth-century Moorish palace in Granada. Those designs inspired him to create the amazing tiling patterns that appear in his art.

Graphic artist M. C. Escher created this butterfly tiling pattern in 1948.

One person who has studied Escher's art is Doris Schattschneider, a math professor at Moravian College in Bethlehem, Pennsylvania. While examining Escher's notebooks, Schattschneider found that Escher had worked out his own mathematical system for classifying tilings. The symbols he used described how portions of the edges of a tile related to each other and to edges of adjacent tiles. The system allowed him to find all the different ways in which he could interlock and color various shapes of identical tiles to create pleasing patterns.

"Escher's interest was not in classifying existing patterns, but in learning the rules that governed such patterns so that he could create his own regular divisions of the plane," Schattschneider explains. Escher's study of geometric shapes, combined with his artistry, were the inspirations for many famous drawings, such as "Butterflies."

The Buckyball Asteroid

You are down on your knees fitting a bunch of triangles and squares into an awesome pattern when you look up and spot a girl wearing a baseball cap and a white soccer shirt with the number "21."

"Hi. What's happening?" she asks casually, as if the two of you were back home, not on some strange asteroid.

"Just tiling the floor," you answer.

"I'm Anita," she says. "My friend Bill over there is looking for Buckyball Field," she adds, pointing to a long-legged, curly haired boy who is kicking a soccer ball. His white soccer shirt has the number "34."

"Did you find it?" Bill asks Anita as he comes running up. "I know this sounds crazy," he explains, "but we're scheduled to play soccer against some space aliens at Buckyball Field, and we don't know where it is."

"I think we're on the wrong asteroid," Anita says with a sigh.

"I bet we could find it from my space capsule," you offer.

Soon you, Anita, and Bill are hanging out in what used to be your bedroom, silently sailing through space.

A sharply pointed shape suddenly appears on the navigation screen. Looking closely, you notice that it has four identical triangular faces. Then other three-dimensional objects come into view. Some have triangular surfaces, like the first one you saw, and others are made up of squares, hexagons, or other polygons.

"Look! There's one made up of twenty triangles," Anita says.

"I see a buckyball!" Bill exclaims, pointing to an object on the screen that looks like a soccer ball. "Quick! Click on it!"

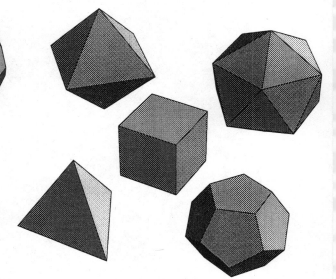

Seven objects appear on the navigation screen.

There are seven objects on the screen. Which one is the buckyball?

[Answer on page 30]

Solid Faces

The shapes pictured on your space capsule's screen are examples of geometric figures known as solids. Solids have three dimensions: length, width, and height. Many solid objects, from pyramids and dice to baseballs and cereal boxes, have shapes that can be described in simple geometric terms.

A solid formed by polygons that enclose a single region of space is called a **polyhedron.** Five of the seven shapes on the screen have surfaces made up of identical, regular polygons, which meet at each corner, or vertex, in exactly the same way.

A regular tetrahedron has four faces, each one an equilateral triangle. Here's what a tetrahedron might look like if it were cut open and unfolded into a flat shape.

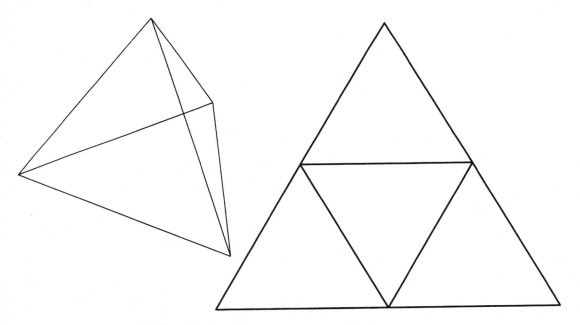

A regular tetrahedron, as seen whole (left) and cut
open and unfolded (right), has four faces, each one an equilateral triangle.

A cube, or regular hexahedron, has six square faces. An octahedron has a surface consisting of eight equilateral triangles. A dodecahedron is made up of twelve pentagons. If you were to cut it into two equal parts, each part would resemble a flower having five pentagon-shaped petals around a central pentagon. An icosahedron has twenty flat surfaces, each one an equilateral triangle.

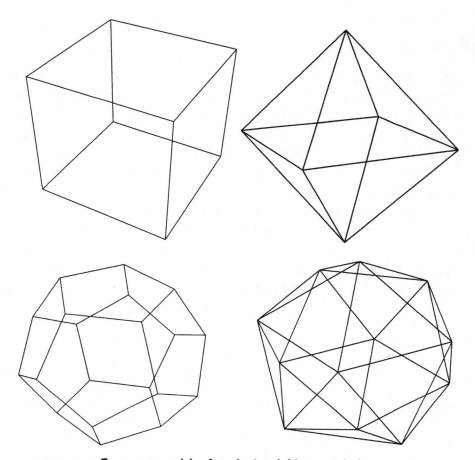

Transparent models of a cube (top left), an octahedron
(top right), a dodecahedron (bottom left), and an icosahedron (bottom right).

More than two thousand years ago, the Greek mathematician Euclid proved that these five objects are the only ones that can be constructed from a single type of regular polygon. Known as the five **Platonic solids,** they are named after the Greek philosopher Plato, who lived around 400 B.C. The Greeks were not the first to study these shapes, however. There is evidence that people in China and in the British Isles knew about them long before Plato's time.

Plato believed that the world was made up of tiny particles consisting of four elements: fire, air, water, and earth. Each particle had the shape of a regular polyhedron. Fire, the lightest and sharpest of the elements, was a tetrahedron. Earth, as the most stable element, consisted of cubes. Water, as the most mobile, was an icosahedron, the regular solid most likely to roll easily. Air was an octahedron, and the dodecahedron represented the entire universe.

Discover an amazing relationship among the vertices, edges, and faces of polyhedra.

YOU WILL NEED

- sheet of paper
- pencil
- ruler
- cube-shaped object such as a game die, a child's building block, or a box
- tetrahedron and other examples of polyhedra, if available (You can make your own tetrahedron and other polyhedra by using toothpicks to represent edges and balls of modeling clay or plasticine as connectors at the vertices to hold the sticks together.)
- soccer ball

WHAT TO DO

1. Divide your sheet of paper into four columns.

2. Label the head of each column as shown below:
   Name of Shape   Faces (F)   Vertices (V)   Edges (E)

3. Under "Name of Shape," write CUBE.

4. Count the number of faces on the cube and record your total under "F."

5. Count the number of vertices and record your total under "V."

6. Count the number of edges and record your total under "E."

7. Record the same information for each polyhedron you have available, including the soccer ball.

8. Look for patterns in the table to find a relationship among the number of vertices, faces, and edges. Hint: Try adding or subtracting various combinations of V, F, and E.

The relationship you are looking for was discovered by Leonhard Euler, an eighteenth-century Swiss mathematician. The rule applies to many different kinds of polyhedra. Can you use it to calculate how many edges a solid with eight faces and twelve vertices must have?

[Answer on page 104.]

The Amazing Buckyball

One of the seven shapes you saw on the space-capsule screen is a **truncated icosahedron.** A regular icosahedron is made up of twenty equilateral triangles that meet at twelve points, or vertices. To create a truncated icosahedron, you chop off each vertex so the twelve vertices turn into twelve pentagons and the twenty equilateral triangles become twenty hexagons. The resulting shape has twenty hexagons and twelve pentagons as its surface, thirty-two faces in all.

Three-dimensional geometry is very useful for describing the arrangement of atoms in different materials. Carbon atoms, for example, can arrange themselves in a pattern that looks like a lot of neatly stacked tetrahedrons. Arranged in this way, carbon atoms form diamonds, one of the hardest materials known. In contrast, when carbon atoms are arranged in hexagonal rings linked together to form vast sheets, they form graphite, a soft material used in lubricants and in pencils. The hexagonal pattern looks like the honeycomb grid you encountered in Trek 2.

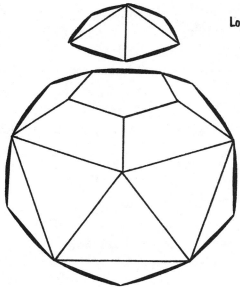

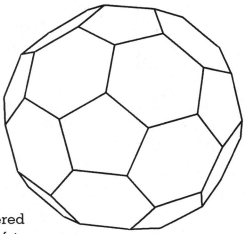

Lopping off one corner of an icosahedron (left) is the first step in creating a truncated icosahedron, or buckyball (right).

In the 1980s, scientists discovered carbon molecules in the shape of truncated icosahedra. Each molecule consists of sixty carbon atoms. They named the molecule buckminsterfullerene, after R. Buckminster Fuller, the engineer, mathematician, and architect who had studied and designed buildings with a similar structure. Now scientists often call these carbon molecules "buckyballs."

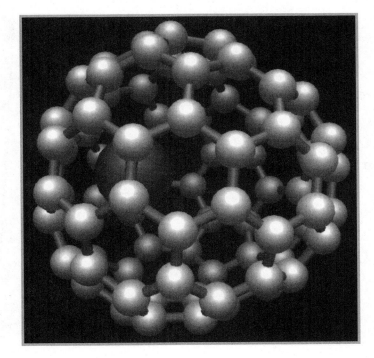

Computer-generated model of a buckyball molecule, which consists of sixty carbon atoms arranged to form a cage. In this example, another atom is trapped inside the cage.

If you count the number of hexagons and pentagons on a soccer ball, you will realize that when you play soccer, you are kicking a truncated icosahedron, also known as a **buckyball**! (Actually, it's not quite a buckyball, because the pentagons and hexagons on a true mathematical buckyball are flat. On a soccer ball they are rounded so that the ball is spherical.)

Can you show that Euler's Rule (page 104) works for a truncated icosahedron?

TRY it

Use paper and scissors to make your own buckyball.

YOU WILL NEED
- copy of the figure on page 31 (Regular copy paper is okay, but slightly heavier paper or card stock is easier to work with.)
- pair of scissors
- roll of tape

WHAT TO DO

1. Cut out the figure along its outer edge.

2. Wherever you see two hexagons sharing a border, fold the paper along the common border. Be sure to make all folds go in the same direction.

3. You will find that the flat sheet easily curls up into a spherelike object, with rings of hexagons surrounding the pentagons.

4. Tape together the borders that meet, and you have a truncated icosahedron! As you assemble it, remember that no two pentagons touch each other directly. Also, each vertex is shared by two hexagons and one pentagon.

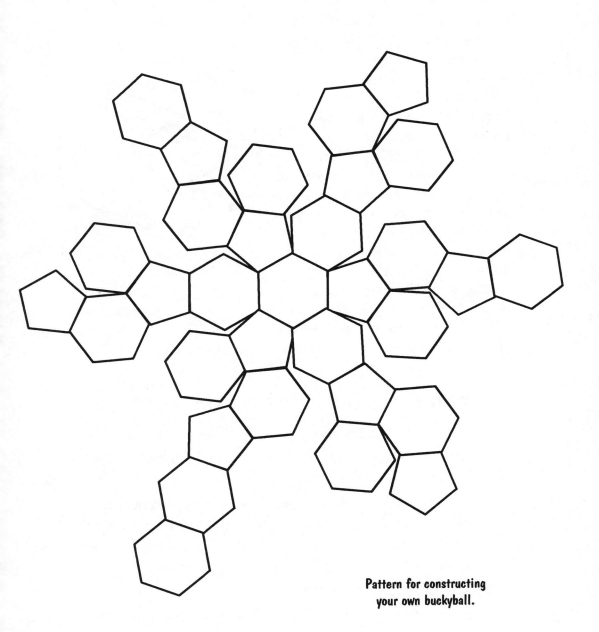

Pattern for constructing
your own buckyball.

Buckyballs Everywhere

Interest in the truncated icosahedron dates back to Archimedes, a Greek mathematician and inventor who lived in the third century B.C. Others probably conceived of the truncated icosahedron even earlier. In fact, objects based on this shape show up in many cultures throughout the world.

Sepak raga, a popular game in Southeast Asia, uses a woven ball that looks similar to a soccer ball. In Mozambique, Madagascar, Zaire, Brazil, and many other countries, local artists weave baskets in patterns with regular hexagonal holes. To turn a flat hexagonal weave into a curved basket shape, the weavers perform a mathematical trick: By reducing the number of strands, they make certain holes pentagonal instead of hexagonal.

Woven ball used for the game *sepak raga.*

ENGINEER FROM "SPACESHIP EARTH"

R. Buckminster Fuller, known as Bucky, lived from 1895 to 1983. He grew up witnessing the invention of the automobile, airplane, radio, television, computer, and atomic bomb.

At a time when many people regarded technology as a means for profit and military superiority, Bucky believed that we could use it to help abolish poverty, hunger, and war. He called our planet "Spaceship Earth" to help convince people that we all need to work together, as the crew of a ship does.

Bucky had an original way of thinking that made it hard for him to fit into the status quo. He was twice expelled from Harvard University. The first time, his family sent him off to a Canadian cotton mill as an apprentice machinist, hoping he would become more mature and responsible. At the mill he became so good at making, installing, and troubleshooting complex machinery that Harvard invited him back. The second time, he was expelled for "showing insufficient interest in his studies." Bucky went to work in a meat-packing house and never completed college.

During World War I he served as a naval officer on a ship with wireless communications and aircraft. Using his mechanical skills and ingenuity, he designed a system for rescuing pilots who had been shot down over the water. The navy rewarded him with an opportunity to study at the U.S. Naval Academy in Annapolis, where he enjoyed courses that went beyond academic theory and dealt with the realities of global communications, air travel, and logistics. The skills he developed would become very important to his future work as an engineer, mathematician, and architect.

One of his next projects was to examine a system of geometry based on the tetrahedron. That lead to the novel building design that made him famous: the geodesic dome.

Geometrically, a geodesic dome is a sphere with a piece sliced off its bottom. Like an icosahedron, a classic geodesic sphere has twenty triangular sides. What makes a geodesic sphere different from an icosahedron is the fact that its triangles are slightly curved and each triangle is subdivided into smaller triangles. The corners of all these smaller triangles are each the same distance from the sphere's center.

Unlike conventional buildings, Fuller's geodesic domes become stronger, lighter, and cheaper per unit of volume as their size increases. They enclose the largest possible volume of space using the smallest possible surface area.

In a geodesic sphere, each face is subdivided into triangles.

Since Bucky patented his design in 1947, more than two hundred thousand geodesic domes have been built around the world, everywhere from high mountaintops to the South Pole. They are the strongest structures ever devised and the most immune to damage from hurricanes and earthquakes.

The U. S. Pavillion (top) at Expo '67 in Montreal was a two-hundred-foot-high version of Buckminster Fuller's geodesic dome. The close-up shows the hexagonal units that make up most of its surface. The dome is now a family-oriented museum called the Biosphere.

The Alien Baseball Field

Puzzler: Why is Trek 4 missing?

Answer: Four is not a Fibonacci number.

Wolk-Stanley 2000

Grasping the computer mouse, you are about to click on the buckyball. Oops! The mouse slips, and you inadvertently click on a different object. Your space capsule zooms toward something that looks like a giant baseball.

"We're landing on an asteroid!" Bill exclaims.

"What's that?" asks Anita, pointing out the window at some markings on the ground. "It's like a baseball diamond!"

"What a weird diamond," Bill says. "The baselines look sort of curved."

As the three of you step outside, a tall, very thin figure approaches.

"Hey, you're late for the game," the alien says.

You gaze in awe at this odd figure, which looks amazingly like the numeral "1."

"Come on," the figure says, leading you to the weird baseball diamond. "It's Digits versus Earthlings; you guys bat first."

As the tall, thin Digit walks over to first base, you spot another strange figure standing near second base: an alien creature shaped like the number "2." What's more, there's a "3" standing at third base, a "4" behind home plate, a "5" at shortstop, and a "6" on the pitcher's mound. The outfield seems to disappear beyond the horizon, but you can make out the top of a "7" in left field. In center field, you see the top of an "8," and the right fielder looks like a "9."

"You first," says Anita, picking up a bat and handing it to you.

The pitcher sends you a slow, easy pitch, and you give the ball a light tap. It's a grounder heading straight toward third. Before you can run, however, the ball curves and ends up rolling across the baseline. What an unfair foul!

When the next pitch comes, you swing and smack the ball toward center field. Instead of landing in the outfield, though, the ball keeps on going until it vanishes over the horizon. You race around the bases, wondering why you don't have to turn very much at each corner. As you approach home plate, the ball you had hit reappears from behind the backstop, just misses the catcher, and flies over the field a second time.

What sort of shape is the baseball diamond, and why doesn't the baseball land?

[Answers follow.]

Lines on a Sphere

Although Earth is roughly spherical, its curvature does not affect the shape of, say, a baseball diamond or a straight road, because the planet is so large.

You would have to take Earth's curvature into account, however, if you were plotting an airplane route from Los Angeles to New York and wanted to find the shortest possible path. The standard rules of geometry on a flat surface would no longer apply. On a small asteroid, the sphere's curvature could even affect the shape of a baseball diamond.

On a flat surface, the shortest path between two points is a straight line. What is the shortest path between two points on a spherical surface?

[Answer follows.]

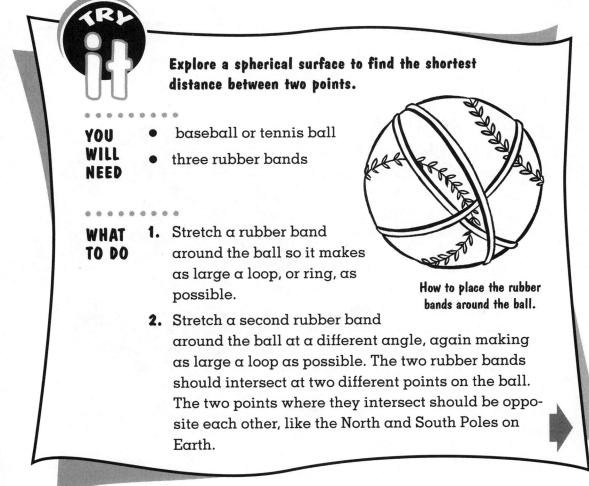

Explore a spherical surface to find the shortest distance between two points.

YOU WILL NEED
- baseball or tennis ball
- three rubber bands

WHAT TO DO

1. Stretch a rubber band around the ball so it makes as large a loop, or ring, as possible.

How to place the rubber bands around the ball.

2. Stretch a second rubber band around the ball at a different angle, again making as large a loop as possible. The two rubber bands should intersect at two different points on the ball. The two points where they intersect should be opposite each other, like the North and South Poles on Earth.

3. Stretch the third rubber band around the ball, again making as wide a ring as possible, and see where it intersects the first two rings. Experiment with putting the band in different positions to see how it can intersect the first two rings in different ways.

4. Pick any two points where the rubber bands intersect. The shortest distance between them on the ball's surface is along the rubber band connecting the two points.

Great Circles and Angles

The circular paths formed by the rubber bands around a ball are called **great circles.** If you were to slice a ball exactly in half, its rim would be a great circle. On Earth, one geographic example of a great circle is the equator. The lines of longitude are great circles that intersect one another at the North Pole and at the South Pole. Great circles are the largest of all circles that can be drawn on the surface of a sphere.

Three great circles divide up the surface of a sphere into various regions, such as the triangle shown.

The shortest distance between two points on a sphere is along the arc of a great circle joining the two points. On any three-dimentional surface, including a sphere, the shortest distance between two points is called a **geodesic.** To find the geodesic between any two points marked on a baseball or a tennis ball, just stretch a rubber band around the ball to form a great circle that passes over both points.

A baseball diamond on a small, spherical asteroid would have baselines that are arcs of great circles. That's why the baselines end up being curved.

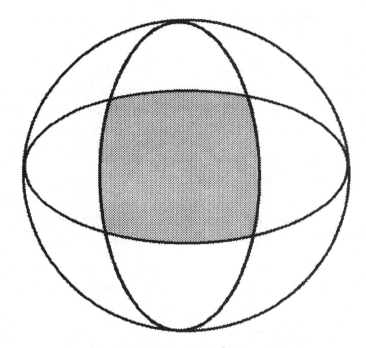

Four great circles intersect to form a square.

Curved baselines are not the only weird things about an asteroid baseball diamond. If you were to measure the angles at the four corners of the diamond, you would get a surprising result. On a flat surface, the angles are each 90 degrees, but on a spherical surface, they are not. Furthermore, the sum of the four angles is 360 degrees on a flat baseball diamond, but not on a sphere. How large are the angles?

[Answer follows.]

Use great circles to make a spherical baseball diamond and measure the angles.

YOU WILL NEED

- soccer ball or other spherical object of similar size
- four large rubber bands (large enough to stretch around the sphere)
- protractor for measuring angles
- paper and pencil

WHAT TO DO

1. Stretch two rubber bands around the sphere so that they both form great circles. The circles will cross at two opposite points on the ball. Try to position the rubber bands so they form angles of about 90 degrees.

2. Add a third rubber band so it forms a great circle but does not intersect either of the two points where the first two rubber bands meet. The three rubber bands should divide the surface of your ball into six triangles (of course, the triangles are curved, not flat).

3. Choose one of the triangles and measure its three inside angles with your protractor. Record your measurements.

4. Add together the three measurements you recorded. The angles in a flat triangle always add up to 180 degrees. On a sphere of a given size, the sum of the angles depends on the size of the triangle. Is your total more than 180 degrees or less than 180 degrees?

5. Add a fourth rubber band, positioned so it forms a great circle *and* at least one four-sided polygon that approximates the shape of a baseball diamond.

6. Measure the four inside angles of your "baseball diamond" from step 5. Record the measurements.

7. Add your four angle measurements. On a flat four-sided baseball diamond the angles add up to 360 degrees. Is your total higher or lower than 360?

[Answers on page 105.]

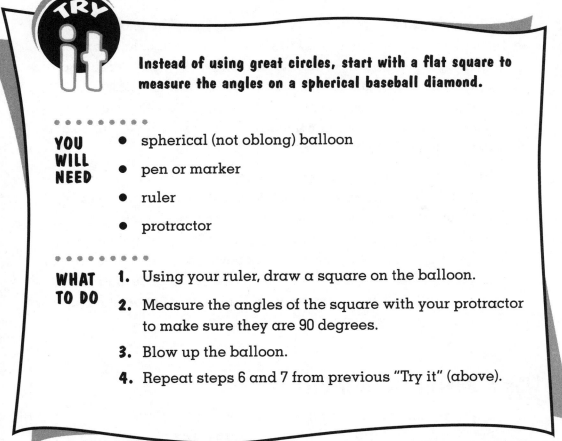

TRY it

Instead of using great circles, start with a flat square to measure the angles on a spherical baseball diamond.

YOU WILL NEED

- spherical (not oblong) balloon
- pen or marker
- ruler
- protractor

WHAT TO DO

1. Using your ruler, draw a square on the balloon.

2. Measure the angles of the square with your protractor to make sure they are 90 degrees.

3. Blow up the balloon.

4. Repeat steps 6 and 7 from previous "Try it" (above).

[Answer on page 105.]

Great Soccer Circles

Study the edges of the pentagons and hexagons on a soccer ball. Try covering the edges with large rubber bands. Are all of the "edge" lines on a soccer ball arcs of great circles?

[Answer on page 105.]

Minipuzzler

A pilot flies due south 100 kilometers, then goes east 100 kilometers, then north 100 kilometers. She ends up right back where she started. Where was her starting point? (Hint: Study a world globe.)

[Answer on page 105.]

• •

SPHERELAND

Pilots and airline route planners covering large distances across the globe have to consider Earth's shape in their calculations. The shortest route from New York to Tokyo, for example, doesn't go directly from east to west along a line of latitude, but actually follows a great circle that passes near the North Pole. Drawn on a flat map, such a route may look curved, but it's really a shortcut for both pilot and passengers!

In fact, spherical geometry plays an important role not just in navigation but also in many other fields. In mathematics it appears in trigonometry, topology, calculus, and other areas. Spherical geometry also has applications in physics, chemistry, crystallography, earth sciences, astronomy, art, technical drawing, industrial design, and engineering. You couldn't put a satellite into orbit around Earth or send a spacecraft to Mars without understanding spherical geometry.

• •

Why a Baseball Can Orbit

Suppose you were standing on an extremely high mountaintop on Earth, and you fired a bullet horizontally. The bullet would travel in an arc, curving downward as it speeds away from the mountain and eventually hitting the ground, pulled by gravity.

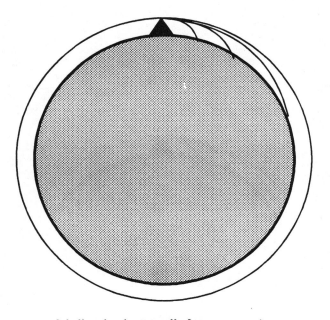

A bullet shot horizontally from a mountaintop
will eventually hit the ground, unless its initial
speed is fast enough to put it in orbit.

A relatively slow bullet would hit the ground near the mountain. Faster bullets would travel farther. If it were fast enough, a bullet could end up going entirely around Earth. Like a little moon or a satellite, it would travel around in its circular orbit again and again. (Be sure to duck before it circles the globe and hits you in the back.)

Using the laws of physics formulated by the English scientist Isaac Newton more than three hundred years ago, it's possible to calculate the necessary speed for an object, such as a bullet or a spacecraft, to go into orbit around Earth or any other spherical body. The speed depends on the object's distance from the sphere's center and its acceleration caused by gravity. A satellite orbiting just above Earth's surface would have to travel at a speed of about 8 kilometers per second to remain in orbit.

A softly thrown baseball moves at about 10 meters per second. A hard-hit baseball can go 40 meters per second or faster. That's fast enough for a ball to go into orbit around a small asteroid!

The Bumpy Bike Path

Puzzler: Why are Treks 6 and 7 missing?
Answer: Fibonacci numbers only, please.

"If you think our baseball field is weird, come and see our roads and tracks," says the tall, thin alien who had been playing first base.

The team of nine Digits leads you, Anita, and Bill down a very bumpy road.

"How do you Digits manage to walk here?" you ask, trying to keep your balance.

"We don't often walk," says Digit One, the tall, thin alien, with a wide grin. "We ride our bikes."

"Yeah, sure," says Anita. "Who could ride a bike on these bumps?"

"Take a look at our bikes," says Digit One, pointing to a nearby hut with a sign.

Bike Shed: Pick Your Wheels

Digit Four opens the door, revealing several odd-looking bikes. "Why don't you try them out," the alien tells you and your two companions. "You might be surprised how smooth the ride can be if your bike suits the road."

Four types of bike wheels: round (top left), elliptical (top right),
square (bottom left), and star-shaped (bottom right).

The first bike you see looks ordinary, but the one beside it has wheels that look like flattened circles, or ellipses. A third bike has square wheels. There's even a bike with star-shaped wheels.

Which of these four bikes will give you the smoothest ride on the bumpy road?

[Answer follows.]

Going Flat

Nobody likes riding a bike with a flat tire. You bump along and don't get very far, and the metal rim on your wheel gets wrecked. If the road itself has evenly spaced bumps of just the right shape, however, flat-sided tires can be the secret to a smooth ride!

Believe it or not, the bumps on the aliens' road are the perfect shape to produce a smooth ride on a square-wheeled bike. It can't be just any old square-wheeled bike, though. Each side of the square tires must be just the right length to fit over one bump, and the wheel's size must be related mathematically to the bump's height.

The bumps on the aliens' road are the shape of upside-down, or inverted, catenaries. A **catenary** is the special shape formed by a chain or a rope hanging loosely between two supports.

A hanging string, fastened at its two ends, forms a catenary shape.

Create your own inverted catenary.

YOU WILL NEED

- piece of string, rope, or chain about 10 inches (25 centimeters) long
- sheet of paper

WHAT TO DO

1. Hold one end of the string in your left hand and the other end in your right hand, each at about the same height.

2. Let the string hang loosely between your hands. It forms a catenary!

3. Carefully lay it down on a sheet of paper without changing the string's shape.

4. Turn the paper so the string forms an upside-down U.

   Now you can picture the cross section of each bump of the alien roadway. A series of such bumps, lined up in a row, would be the perfect surface on which to ride a square-wheeled bike.

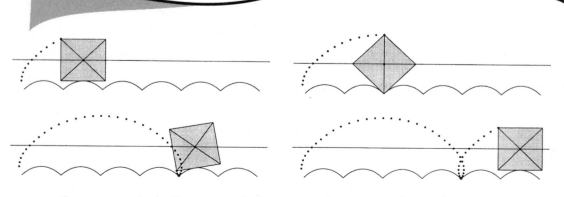

How a square wheel rolls over a roadbed consisting of a sequence of inverted catenaries.

TRIKING AROUND

Stan Wagon, a mathematician at Macalester College in St. Paul, Minnesota, has built a real tricycle with square wheels, which he rides on a road of inverted catenaries.

Wagon first learned about traveling on square wheels when he saw an exhibit at the Exploratorium in San Francisco. The exhibit featured a pair of square wheels joined by an axle riding over an inverted catenary roadbed. Intrigued by the demonstration, Wagon decided to build a square-wheeled bike he could actually ride himself.

"As soon as I saw it could be done, I had to do it," Wagon says. The bike was tricky to build, and he ended up with an unusual kind of tricycle. He also had to construct an inverted catenary surface on which to ride it. Wagon's square-wheeled trike is now on display at the Macalester College science center.

"It rides like a normal bike, though steering is difficult," says Wagon. If you turn the square wheels too much, they get out of sync with the inverted catenaries.

Having two front wheels and one back wheel helps make it easier to ride the trike in a straight line. If you had a bicycle instead, you would need to turn the wheel now and then to help keep your balance, and that's hard to do with square wheels on a bumpy road.

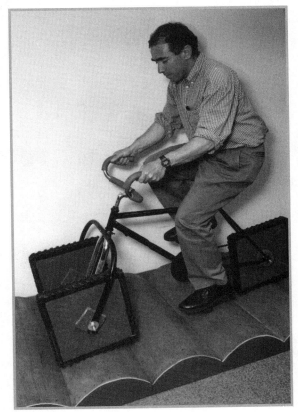

Stan Wagon's square-wheeled trike in action.

Make a square-wheeled unicycle for a two-dimensional, inverted catenary road.

YOU WILL NEED

- four copies of the inverted catenary shown below (trace, or use a copy machine)

- scissors

- tape

- four toothpicks, trimmed so each one has the same length as a side of the square shown below

WHAT TO DO

1. Cut and tape together the inverted catenaries so they form a "roadway," as shown below.

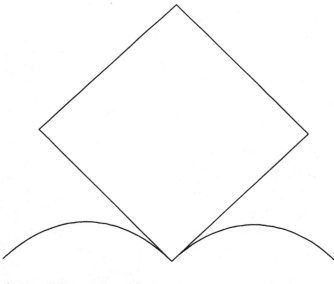

Matching the length of the side of a square wheel to the length of one unit of an inverted-catenary road.

2. Arrange the four toothpicks into a square and connect the corners with tape to create a square wheel.

3. Pretend that your square wheel is a unicycle, and roll it along the inverted catenary road you made.

HOW IT WORKS The curved-line segment of each catenary is the same length as each toothpick, so if you start with one corner of the square at the beginning of the road, each corner will end up at a point between two catenaries as you roll the wheel along.

Different Roads for Different Wheels

It turns out that wheels in the shape of other regular polygons, such as pentagons and hexagons, also ride smoothly over curves made up of inverted catenaries. The number of sides on the polygon affects the road's shape: as the number of sides increases, the catenary segments get shorter and flatter. For a polygon with an infinite number of sides (in effect, a circle), the best "curve" is a straight, horizontal line.

Triangular wheels don't work, though. As a triangle rolls over one catenary, it ends up bumping into the next catenary.

A triangular wheel doesn't work because its points get stuck in the roadbed.

Mathematicians have found roads for some other wheel shapes, such as an ellipse (which looks like a flattened circle), a rosette (like a flower with four petals), or a teardrop. They can even start with a road profile and find the shape that runs smoothly across it. A sawtooth road, for example, requires a wheel pasted together from pieces of an equiangular spiral (sort of a cross between a flower and a star shape).

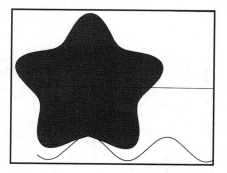

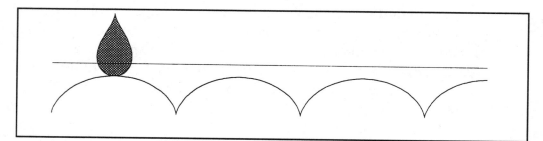

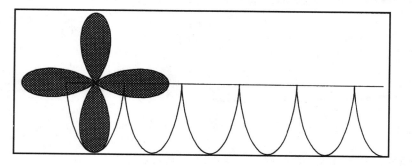

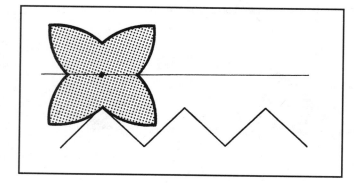

Various combinations of wheel shape and road profile would give you a smooth ride.

So far, no one has ever found a road-and-wheel combination in which the road has the same shape as the wheel. That's an intriguing challenge for mathematicians!

ROLLING WITH REULEAUX

A circular wheel isn't the only type of wheel that would ride smoothly over a flat, horizontal road.

Consider the problem of making a manhole cover with a shape that won't let it fall through an opening in the street. One answer is to use a circular lid that is slightly larger than the circular hole it covers. The lid can't slip through because it's wider than the hole, no matter which way you turn it. A circle has the same width all the way around.

In contrast, an oval is longer than it is wide. You can always find a way to slip an oval lid through an oval hole that is the same size or slightly smaller. That's also true of a square cover or a hexagonal cover.

Is a circle the only shape that works safely as a manhole cover? Is it the only shape that makes a smooth-riding wheel on a flat surface? No! The Reuleaux triangle also works. It is named after engineer Franz Reuleaux, who was a teacher in Berlin, Germany, more than a hundred years ago.

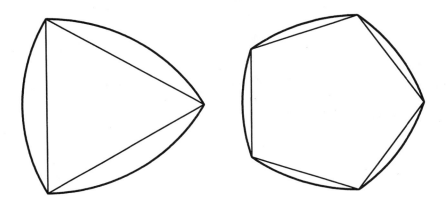

Both the Reuleaux triangle (left) and the Reuleaux pentagon (right) have curved sides.

You might find an example of a Reuleaux triangle in your medicine cabinet. If you turn a bottle of Nyquil or Pepto-Bismol upside down, the shape you see looks like a Reuleaux triangle. If you try rolling one of these bottles on its side, you'll find that it rolls as smoothly as a round bottle.

One way to draw a Reuleaux triangle is to start with an equilateral triangle, which has three sides of equal length. Place the pointed end of a pair of compasses at one corner of the triangle and stretch the arms until the pencil reaches another corner. Then draw an arc between two corners of the triangle. Draw two more arcs centered on the triangle's other corners.

This "curved triangle," as Reuleaux called it, has a constant width—just like a circle. It can roll smoothly on a flat surface, like a circular wheel.

In fact, you can make a manhole cover or a wheel out of any regular polygon with an odd number of sides. Beginning with a five-sided shape, for example, you can construct a rounded pentagonal shape with a constant width.

Any object with such a cross section would roll smoothly across your kitchen floor or down the street.

Pi in the Sky

After a day of baseball and bicycling with the Digit aliens, you are growing hungry.

"Join us for a pie feast!" says Digit Three, leading you to a very long picnic table. Standing at one end of the table, you can't even see all the way to the other end; the table seems to go on forever.

The nine Digits scramble off into the woods. Moments later, Digit Three reappears with a humongous pizza and sits down in a special chair at the head of the table. Then Digit One appears with a turkey pie and sits on the long bench to the left of Three. Four comes along with a spinach pie and sits beside One.

More Digits emerge from the woods, each carrying a different kind of pie. Another One sits beside Four with a cherry pie. Then come Five with a blueberry pie, Nine with a peach pie, and Two with an apple pie.

As Six arrives and takes a seat beside Two, the Digits invite you, Anita, and Bill to sit across the table. More Digits keep coming, and they start passing around slices of pie to share.

"How many of you are coming?" you ask.

"Everyone is invited, and our current population is 206,158,430,000," says Three, who is still sitting at the head of the table. "Our population keeps growing because we never die, and we keep on having babies."

As you contemplate the idea of eating pie with more than 206 billion Digits, Bill looks up and down the row of Digits on the bench. He gets a befuddled look on his face. Anita studies the row of Digits and breaks out laughing.

What is so funny about the seating order?

[Answer follows.]

The Digits of Pi

The pie-eating Digits are seated in the same order as the digits of a mysterious and special number in mathematics known as **pi.** As you may know, pi is the ratio of a circle's **circumference** (the distance around the circle) to its **diameter** (the distance across, passing through the center). No matter how large or small the circle, its circumference divided by its diameter equals 3.14159265 . . . : the number we call pi. The digits to the right of the decimal point continue without end, following no particular pattern. The mathematical symbol for pi is the Greek letter "π."

Because pi is an **irrational number,** it can't be expressed exactly as a fraction, such as ¾ or 22/7. It would take an infinite sequence of decimal digits to state the number exactly. So if all the digits of pi were lined up along the bench of a picnic table, the table would have to be infinitely long. The "current population" of alien Digits, however, is only 206,158,430,000. That's the number of consecutive digits of pi that mathematicians have calculated so far.

Digit Hunters

Calculating the value of pi has been a fascinating challenge since ancient times.

In about 1650 B.C., the Egyptian scribe Ahmes wrote out a set of math problems. In one problem, he assumed that the area of a circular field with a diameter of 9 units is the same as the area of a square with a side of 8 units. So, for the Egyptians, this meant that pi was equal to 4 times $\frac{8}{9}$ times $\frac{8}{9}$, which is 3.16049...—a little less than its true value.

More than a thousand years later, the Greek mathematician and physicist Archimedes (287–212 B.C.) found the value 3.1419 for pi. His estimate was off by less than three ten-thousandths, and the numbering system he used to calculate it didn't even have a symbol for 0!

In the fifth century A.D., the Chinese astronomer Tsu Ch'ungchih and his son Tsu Keng-chih figured out that pi is about $\frac{355}{113}$, or 3.1415929. This is only about eight millionths of a percent more than the true value of pi, which is 3.1415926....

Meanwhile, throughout the first millennium, the Romans and others were working with less accurate values of pi. In 1220, Fibonacci wrote that pi is approximately $\frac{864}{275}$, which is about 3.1418. That's close to the value used much earlier by the ancient Greeks.

Soon after that, the Europeans began making great strides in zeroing in on the true value of pi, expressed in decimal digits. In 1585 a Dutch mathematician rediscovered 3.1415929 without knowing that the Chinese had already found this value more than a thousand years earlier. Eight years later, another Dutch mathematician accurately calculated the first 15 decimal digits of pi, and then a German found the first 35 digits.

By 1722 a Japanese mathematician had calculated 40 digits. In the early 1800s a mathematician in China found 100 digits, and an Austrian mathematician correctly calculated 140 digits of pi. With the advent of computers in the twentieth century, the pi world's record climbed to thousands of digits, then millions, then billions!

DECIMAL DIGITS OF PI: WORLD RECORD

Number of decimal digits: 206,158,430,000

Computed by: Yasumasa Kanada and coworkers, University of Tokyo

Year: 1999

Amount of computer time required: 37 hours

Most common digit among first 200 billion: 8 (appears 20,000,291,044 times)

Least common digit: 6 (appears 19,999,869,180 times)

Last known digit: 4

TRY it

Calculate pi using the classic method of the Greeks.

The method involves measuring the perimeters of two polygons (in this case, hexagons)—one **inscribed** inside a circle and the other **circumscribed** around the outside of the circle, as shown on page 59. The circle is larger than one polygon and smaller than the other, so you can measure the perimeter of each polygon and calculate the average of the two perimeters to estimate the circumference of the circle.

Because any circle's circumference divided by its diameter equals pi, your estimated circumference divided by the diameter is an approximation of pi.

A circle shown with an inscribed hexagon (shaded) and a circumscribed hexagon.

YOU WILL NEED

- ruler
- pencil and paper
- calculator (optional)

WHAT TO DO

1. Measure the length of one side of the inscribed (smaller) hexagon.

2. Multiply your answer by 6 to calculate the perimeter of the inscribed hexagon.

3. Measure one side of the circumscribed (larger) hexagon.

4. Multiply your answer by 6 to find the perimeter of the circumscribed hexagon.

5. Since the circle is larger than one hexagon and smaller than the other, find the average of the two perimeters to estimate the circumference of the circle. To calculate this average, add your total from step 2 and your total from step 4, then divide by 2. Call your answer "c" —the estimated circumference of the circle.

6. Measure the diameter of the circle, labeled "d."

7. Calculate c/d to get your estimate for pi.

[Answers on page 105.]

The larger the number of sides on the two polygons, the more accurate is the approximation of pi. In the diagram on page 59, the polygons are hexagons. Archimedes used ninety-six-sided polygons. By the 1600s, mathematicians were using polygons with millions of sides to find more and more digits of pi!

Targeting Pi

Here's another way to obtain an approximate value of pi.

Suppose you have a square dartboard on which you've drawn a circle that just fits within the square. You throw darts so poorly that they land randomly all over the square.

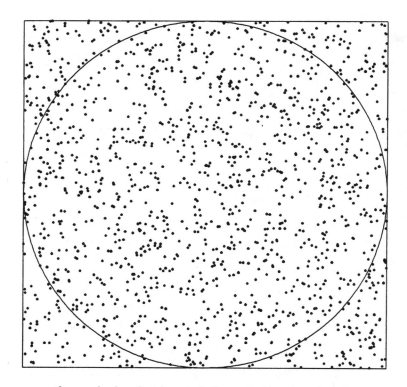

Square dartboard with a circle for estimating the value of pi.

The circle has a diameter that is exactly the same as the width of the square. Divide the number of darts that landed within the circle by the total number of darts that were used. The answer you get is roughly one-quarter the value of pi. Just multiply this answer by 4 to get an estimate of the value of pi.

The more darts you throw (and the less accurate your aim), the better your estimate gets.

Back to the Alien Digits

After the pie feast, the Digits invite Anita, Bill, and you to spend the night with them camping out under the stars.

Soon the sky grows dark, and the Digits give each of you a sleeping bag. They line up their own sleeping bags in the same order they had sat in at the picnic table: 314159 . . . . You and your friends set your sleeping bags nearby. Then, lying comfortably on your backs, all of you gaze up at a sky full of stars.

"Time to look for pi in the sky," says Three, handing each of you an object that looks like the protractor you use in geometry class for measuring angles.

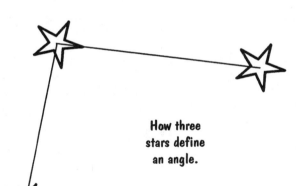

How three stars define an angle.

"Now, pick any three bright stars," says One. "Use your protractor to measure the angle they form, like this."

"Now tell us the measurement of your angle," says Four.

Positioning your protractor, you measure an angle formed by three stars.

"Twenty-two degrees," you report.

Anita reports, "Ninety-eight degrees."

"Mine is 123 degrees," says Bill.

"Good," says One. "The numbers 22 and 98 are both divisible by 2. The numbers 22 and 123 have no common factor except 1. The third pair of numbers, 98 and 121, also have no common factors.

"So what?" asks Bill. "What do star angles have to do with pi?"

[Answer follows.]

SPYING PI IN THE SKY

The Digits plan to estimate pi using a method introduced by British scientist Robert Matthews in 1995.

The method is based on the fact that for any two whole numbers chosen from a large, random collection of numbers, the probability that the two numbers have no common factors is $6/\pi^2$, which equals about 0.61. In other words, any two numbers greater than 1 have about a 61 percent chance of having no common factors (except the number 1, which is a factor of any whole number).

For example, if you factor the numbers 22, 98, and 123, you get:

$$22 = 2 \times 11$$
$$98 = 2 \times 7 \times 7$$
$$123 = 3 \times 41$$

The numbers 22 and 98 have the number 2 as a common factor. The pair 22 and 123 has no common factor except 1. The pair 98 and 123 also has no common factors.

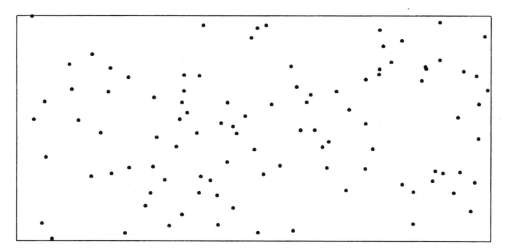

A computer's random-number generator can be used to create
a map showing a hundred stars scattered haphazardly across the sky.

Matthews used the positions of stars in the sky as his source for generating random numbers. He measured the different angles formed by the hundred brightest stars visible in the sky to come up with a million pairs of numbers. He then used a computer to check each pair of numbers for factors.

Calculating the percentage of number pairs with common factors allowed him to estimate that pi has the value 3.12772. That's within 0.5 percent of the actual value of pi. In this strange way, he really did find pi in the sky!

Galactic Gridlock

It's daytime when you awaken on the Digits' asteroid. Beside you, Anita and Bill are just starting to stir. Most of the Digits are still asleep, but Eight is already up and walking toward you.

"Good morning! I have a great story to tell," Eight says.

Anita, Bill, and you sit down with Eight, facing one another in a square formation.

"Long, long ago, in a galaxy far, far away, I lived where everything was perfectly predictable and regular," Eight says. "All of my neighbors were perfect cubes, like myself."

Noticing Bill's puzzled look, he explains, "Eight equals 2 cubed, or $2 \times 2 \times 2$. My next-door neighbor was 64, which is 4 cubed, or $4 \times 4 \times 4$. Each of us lived in a cubic house on a square plot of land, and the streets lined up like a giant checkerboard. The ground was perfectly flat, of course."

"I live in a town like that on Earth," says Anita. "There are no hills in Cedarville, and all the streets form a grid."

"Ah, but when you stand on Earth and look up at the night sky, the stars are scattered randomly, just as they are here in Pi Land," Eight says. "In my native galaxy, all the stars are lined up in the form of a three-dimensional grid, perfectly arranged in evenly spaced rows, columns, and stacks. We call it the Cubic Grid Galaxy."

"I'd like to see that!" exclaims Bill.

"You can. All you need is a laser navigator. When I left the Cubic Grid to seek my fortune here in the Random Universe, I brought along a bunch of them."

Handing you a sleek black box with a silver button, Eight continues, "This laser navigator will beam you straight to the Cubic Grid Galaxy. When you get there, press the 'zoom' button and it will send you in one of six directions, chosen randomly: left, right, up, down, forward, or backward. You can explore the galaxy by zooming randomly from star to star."

"Sounds awesome," Anita says.

"One warning, though: if your route crosses over and through itself to form a knot, you will enter a strange new world," Eight cautions.

Before you know it, Anita, Bill, and you are back inside your space capsule, speedily approaching the Cubic Grid Galaxy. You can see the galaxy glittering ahead, like a diamond in the sky! Then you enter the giant diamond and begin whizzing by row after row and column after column of brightly shining stars.

When you press the "zoom" button on the laser navigator, your space capsule shoots straight ahead and begins orbiting the nearest star. Then you press "zoom" again, and this time you head for the star to the left. You notice, however, that the laser navigator never lets you visit the same star twice.

You are having great fun zooming from star to star when suddenly you recall Digit Eight's strange warning. What are the chances that your random route will form a knot?

[Answer follows.]

Random Walks, Random Knots

Have you ever left a necklace or a piece of string lying around on a table in a jumbled heap? There's a good chance that it will form a knot when you pick it up again, especially if it has been jostled a little. The same thing can happen to a garden hose left in an untidy pile on the ground.

Mariners and rock climbers know about that problem, so they take great care to store their ropes in ways that prevent accidental knotting. Because we are used to taking some effort to tie a knot, the unintended formation of knots in ropes, hoses, strings, and necklaces can be both frustrating and puzzling.

Topologists—mathematicians who study shapes—have investigated the spontaneous formation of knots using a three-dimensional grid that resembles the Cubic Grid Galaxy. They imagine a walker standing at one point, or a vertex, of the cubic grid. The walker steps randomly from one vertex to the next in any one of the six directions available from a given point.

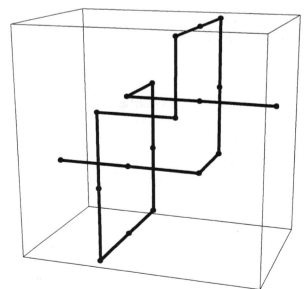

Example of a short, self-avoiding random walk in three dimensions.

Since the path is chosen randomly, perhaps by rolling a six-sided die to determine the direction of each step, topologists call the walker's path a **random walk.** When the walker is not allowed to revisit the same vertex a second time, the path is called a **self-avoiding random walk.**

Mathematicians and scientists use random walks as models for explaining a variety of natural phenomena, including the shapes and folds of polymers, the chainlike molecules that make up plants and animals. Plant and animal by-products such as wood, petroleum, and plastics are also made of polymers. The DNA molecules in our own bodies are polymers, too.

Polymers consist of long chains of "monomer" units. The chains twist and turn and cross over their own paths like a tangled string of beads. Each bead on a string, and each monomer in a polymer chain, is like one step in a random walk. In fact, they are like self-avoiding random walks. No two beads can occupy the same place on a necklace, and neither can two monomers on a polymer chain.

In 1988, a mathematician at Florida State University and a chemist at the University of Toronto used a self-avoiding random walk as a model for a polymer chain. They proved that the longer the chain or random walk, the greater its chance of forming a knot. Similarly, if you zoom to enough stars in the cubic galaxy, your route is almost certain to form a knot.

Walking a Line

Imagine yourself balanced on a tightrope high above the ground. You can take steps only forward or backward. Similarly, in a one-dimensional random walk, the walker is confined to a long, narrow path and can step in either of two directions. Tossing a coin would be one random way to determine whether to step forward (heads) or backward (tails).

You can keep track of a one-dimensional walk by plotting a graph that shows how far away you are from your starting point after each toss of a coin. If your first toss is heads, you end up one step forward from the start. If you toss heads again, you end up two steps forward. A third toss of heads would bring you three steps forward. If your fourth toss were tails, you would step back to the spot two steps away from the start.

This graph shows the results of a one-dimensional random walk. The horizontal axis represents the number of steps taken, and the vertical axis shows how many steps you are away from your starting point if you start at zero. Steps in the forward direction are positive (upward) and steps backward are negative (downward).

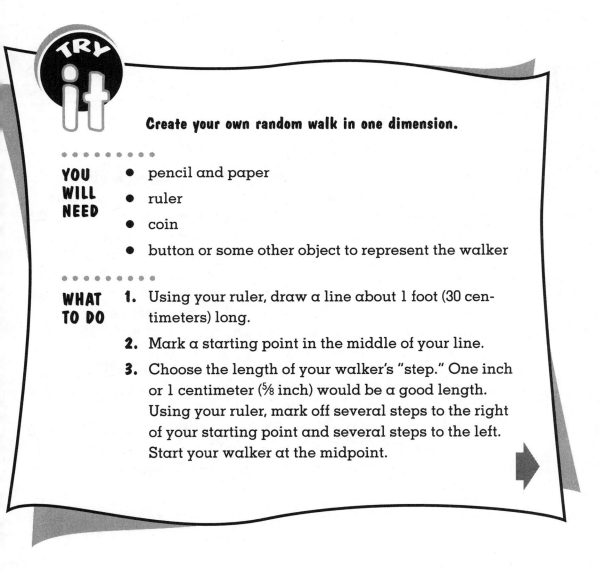

TRY it

Create your own random walk in one dimension.

YOU WILL NEED

- pencil and paper
- ruler
- coin
- button or some other object to represent the walker

WHAT TO DO

1. Using your ruler, draw a line about 1 foot (30 centimeters) long.

2. Mark a starting point in the middle of your line.

3. Choose the length of your walker's "step." One inch or 1 centimeter (⅝ inch) would be a good length. Using your ruler, mark off several steps to the right of your starting point and several steps to the left. Start your walker at the midpoint.

4. Flip the coin. If it lands on heads, move your walker one step to the right from your starting point. If it lands on tails, move it one step to the left.

5. Flip the coin again and go one step to the right for heads or one step to the left for tails, starting from the point where your walker landed after the previous coin flip.

6. Continue flipping the coin and marking the walker's position.

The more times you flip the coin, the farther the walker is likely to stray from the original starting point. Mathematicians have shown that the most probable distance (in steps) from the start equals the square root of the number of steps taken to get to that point.

In other words, after tossing the coin nine times, the walker is likely to be the square root of nine, or three, steps from the start. Of course, your walker may be two steps, four steps, or some other distance from the start, but if you repeat the experiment enough times, the walker's most probable distance from the start (after each nine tosses of the coin) will be three steps.

Does your walker at any time return to its original starting point? Mathematicians have proved that a random walker going back and forth along a line will eventually return to the start.

This might sound like a good strategy for anyone who is lost on a tightrope: just take steps at random in either direction, and you will end up where you started, though it could take longer than a lifetime to get there!

Walking on a Grid

It's easy to extend the random-walk model to two dimensions: Take steps to the north, south, east, or west, randomly choosing the direction of each step with equal probability. Instead of flipping a coin, you could toss a four-sided die.

You can imagine this walk going from vertex to vertex on an infinite checkerboard. If such a walk continues for long enough, the walker is certain to touch every vertex and also to make a return visit to the starting point.

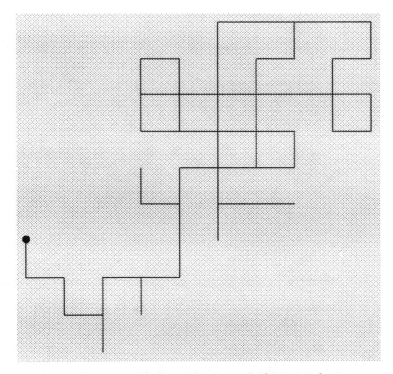

A two-dimensional walk on a square grid, shown step by step.

Record a random walk in two dimensions.

YOU WILL NEED

- sheet of graph paper (or draw your own grid with pencil, paper, and a ruler)
- die (you can use a regular six-sided die, but a tetrahedral die is even better, because you need only four sides)
- pencil

WHAT TO DO

1. Mark a vertex somewhere near the middle of your grid as your starting point. Each roll of the die will determine the direction you take—right, left, up, or down—to one of the four vertices closest to your starting point.

2. Roll the die to determine your direction: If you roll a 1, step up; a 2, step right; a 3, step down; a 4, step left. If you use a six-sided die and roll a 5 or a 6, ignore it and roll again.

3. Draw your route on the grid as you travel. This is not a self-avoiding random walk, so you are allowed to return to a vertex you have already visited.

4. Observe your path. Does it suggest any sort of pattern?

   If you take enough random steps, you will eventually return to your starting point. In fact, an infinitely long random walk will visit every point on the grid an infinite number of times!

5. Repeat steps 2 and 3, but this time take a self-avoiding random walk. In other words, if the direction determined by rolling your die would take you to a vertex you have already visited, stay put and roll again. How does the route of your self-avoiding path compare with your first path? Could you get stuck in a dead end with no place to move?

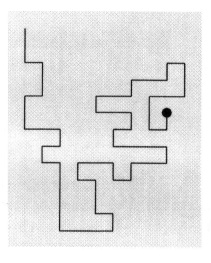

Example of a two-dimensional, self-avoiding random walk.

[Answers on page 105.]

Wandering in Space

In three dimensions, a walker can go forward or backward in addition to left, right, up, or down. Even after taking infinitely many steps, however, the chance of returning to the starting point at any time is only about one in three. There's so much space available in three dimensions that a walker has more chance of wandering far afield than in one or two dimensions.

In fact, the mathematics of a three-dimensional random walk affords an important lesson for anyone who is lost in space. Unless you happen to make it home again within your first few steps, you're likely to end up lost forever. There are simply too many ways to wander off.

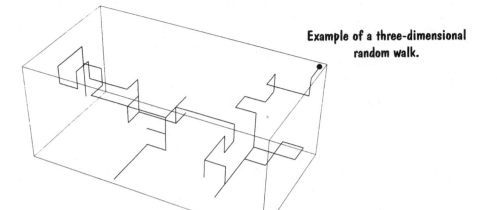

Example of a three-dimensional random walk.

TRY it

Building a large cubic grid takes a lot of work, but the larger your "cubic galaxy," the longer the random walk you can take. Try taking a self-avoiding random walk.

YOU WILL NEED

- connector sticks for constructing a cubic grid (You can use toothpicks and connect them with marshmallows, balls of soft clay, or small Styrofoam balls. Another option is to build a grid with K'nex or with Tinkertoys if you have plenty of pieces. To form a large enough grid, try to have at least sixty marshmallows or other connectors and at least a hundred toothpicks or other sticks that are all the same length.)

- small stickers for marking each vertex you visit

- six-sided die

**WHAT
TO DO**

1. Build a cubic grid by connecting the sticks at 90-degree angles.

2. Pick a vertex near the middle of the grid as your starting point, and mark it with two stickers.

3. Roll the die and move to a neighboring vertex according to the following directions: if you roll a 1, move one step up; if you roll a 2, move to the right; a 3, move down; a 4, move left; a 5, move forward (away from yourself); a 6, move backward (toward yourself).

4. Mark the new vertex with a sticker.

5. Continue rolling the die and moving accordingly. Each time you visit a vertex, mark it with a sticker.

   This is a self-avoiding random walk, so you may not visit the same vertex twice. If your roll would take you to a vertex that is already marked, ignore it and roll again. Also, if you reach an edge of your grid and you roll a number that would take you off the grid, ignore it and roll again.

RANDOM QUIVERS

In the early nineteenth century, British botanist Robert Brown traveled around the world collecting plant specimens. He found that certain pollen grains were transparent when examined under a microscope, and he could see distinct particles inside individual grains. Under a microscope these particles appeared to be in continuous motion, zigzagging randomly about.

Brown's experiments with soot and other types of microscopic particles suspended in water revealed a similar quivering movement. Scientists later suggested that the quivering is caused by the movements of the molecules making up the liquid, and they called this phenomenon "Brownian" motion.

In 1905, Albert Einstein showed mathematically how tiny, randomly moving molecules can budge particles large enough to be observable under a microscope. Molecules of a liquid are in constant motion. Each molecule travels in a straight line until it collides with a particle and bounces away, like a billiard ball. At any given moment, large numbers of molecules can strike a single particle so that each impact shoves the particle in a particular direction. The combined impacts produce more force in some directions than in others, giving the particle a net shove in one direction.

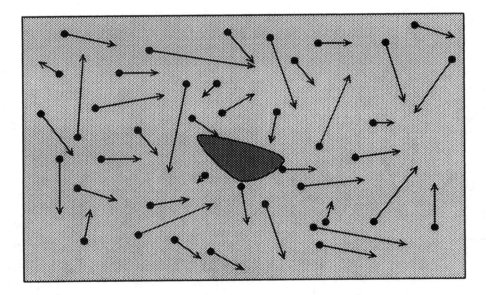

Tiny molecules moving in random directions at different speeds (black dots and arrows) collide with a floating particle (shaded), causing it to move about haphazardly.

The haphazard paths of tiny particles suspended in a liquid are random, like the movements of a three-dimensional random walk!

Hyperspace Hangout

Y ou are zooming randomly from star to star when suddenly a buzzer sounds, a siren goes off, and the lights in your space capsule begin flashing. Your computer display shows a line in a complicated, knotted pattern.

WOLK-STANLEY 2000

You feel a little scared but excited as you recall Eight's warning: "If your route crosses over and through itself to form a knot, you will enter a strange new world."

"Entering hyperspace," a voice blares from your radio speaker.

A large cube appears on your screen, with a black hole in each of its sides. You click on one of the black holes, and it grows so large on the screen that you can see the inside of the cube. Strangely, it looks just like the inside of your space capsule!

Turning from the screen, you gaze around the room—your space capsule—and realize that its shape is now a perfect cube. Each wall even has a black hole, and so do the ceiling and the floor!

Anita goes over to the hole on the left and steps through. The instant she exits, she reappears through the hole on the wall to your right.

Bill bends over to examine the hole in the floor. When he dangles his left leg down through the hole, you see his left foot dangling down from the ceiling.

Where in the universe are you?

[Answer follows.]

Beyond Three Dimensions

You have entered **hyperspace.** Ordinary space is three-dimensional. Hyperspace is the term that mathematicians use to describe four-dimensional space.

When topologists started going beyond our three-dimensional world to explore geometric forms in four or more dimensions, they found it tricky to describe and classify the new forms they discovered. They introduced the term **manifold** to describe a certain type of common higher-dimensional object, in which opposite sides may sometimes be connected through a higher dimension. The cube of your space capsule is one example of such a manifold, because going out through one side brings you back in through the opposite side.

To create a three-dimensional manifold, you could connect the opposite sides of a two-dimensional square or rectangle. To create a four-dimensional manifold, you would somehow connect the opposite sides of a three-dimensional cube. Your cubic space capsule is an example of a four-dimensional manifold!

TRY it

Turn a two-dimensional rectangle into a three-dimensional manifold that looks like a doughnut.

Connecting the opposite sides of a two-dimensional object to create a three-dimensional manifold helps you imagine how you might be able to do something similar with a three-dimensional object. If you could somehow glue together the opposite sides of a six-sided cube, you could create a four-dimensional manifold.

YOU WILL NEED

- sheet of aluminum foil about 4 inches by 11 inches (10 centimeters by 27 centimeters); if you don't have aluminum foil, you can try using paper

- tape

WHAT TO DO

1. Fasten together the two longer sides of your rectangular sheet of aluminum or paper, forming a **cylinder** or tube. You might want to wrap the foil or paper around a cardboard tube to get the right shape before joining the sides together.

How to make a torus from a rectangular sheet.

2. Curve the tube you made in the previous step into a ring, and tape together the two ends of the cylinder, forming a hollow doughnut. The mathematical name for this shape is a **torus.**

From Video Games to Tic-Tac-Toe

Many video games operate like manifolds in order to keep a figure on the screen. When a game figure moves off the right side of the screen, it reappears at the left. When it moves off the top edge, it reappears at the bottom. In effect, the screen's edges have been "glued" together. It's as if the screen were bent around to form a doughnut, or torus.

You're probably used to playing games like tic-tac-toe on a flat surface. Imagine what would happen if a 3-by-3 tic-tac-toe game board were on the surface of a torus instead.

In the game shown below, neither X nor O has three squares in a row, so neither wins. If the board were turned into a torus, however, there would be new ways to have three in a row. What if side A were glued to side B? Would that make X or O win the game?

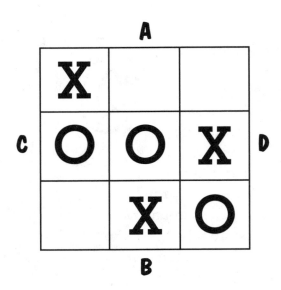

[Answer follows.]

Neither X nor O is the winner in the standard tic-tac-toe game shown on page 80. Figure out whether X or O would win if the tic-tac-toe board were turned into a cylinder or torus, and you applied the same rule for winning.

YOU WILL NEED

- pencil
- sheet of paper
- ruler or straight edge (optional)

WHAT TO DO

1. Turn your sheet of paper into a big tic-tac-toe board so the edges of the game board are the edges of the sheet of paper.

2. Copy the game on page 80 onto your sheet of paper and label the sides A, B, C, and D, as shown.

3. Bend your sheet of paper into a tube so that side A meets side B, with the game facing outward.

4. Notice that three of the X's now form a diagonal line, so X wins the game!

5. In a torus, sides C and D also would meet. To see how the squares would line up, make your sheet of paper flat again, then bend it so C meets D. Look for three X's in a row or three O's in a row to determine the winner.

A tic-tac-toe board wrapped around the outside surface of a cylinder.

[Answers on page 106.]

Escaping a Traffic Jam

Imagine that you are traveling on a four-lane highway. You enter a tunnel and get stuck behind a huge, slow truck. You would like to pass the truck, but you are not allowed to change lanes inside the tunnel. You are free to move only in one dimension, so you creep along behind the truck.

Now that you've reached the end of the tunnel, you can change lanes to pass the truck. You are now able to move in two dimensions.

Then you come to a traffic jam where all the lanes are full of cars and trucks inching along slowly because of highway construction. Travel is blocked in two dimensions, and you wish you could escape to a third dimension and fly up and over the traffic.

What if your car turned into a helicopter, and you could escape the traffic, but a huge storm came along so you couldn't move safely forward or backward, right or left, up or down? Wouldn't it be great to be able to travel in a fourth dimension, untouched by the storm?

From Point to Hypercube

By moving an object in any dimension, you can create an object in the next dimension. Here is how to move from a point to a line segment to a square to a cube to a four-dimensional hypercube:

- A point has zero dimensions.

- Moving a point in a straight line generates a line segment. A line segment is a fundamental one-dimensional object.

- Shifting a line segment at right angles to its length generates a square. A square is a basic two-dimensional object.

- Moving the square at right angles to its plane produces a cube, a basic three-dimensional object.

- What would appear if you could move a cube in a fourth direction, at right angles to all of its edges? The result would be a hypercube, with sixteen corners. It is also called a tesseract, a term sometimes used by science-fiction writers, such as Robert Heinlein in his story "—And He Built a Crooked House" and Madeleine L'Engle in *A Wrinkle in Time*.

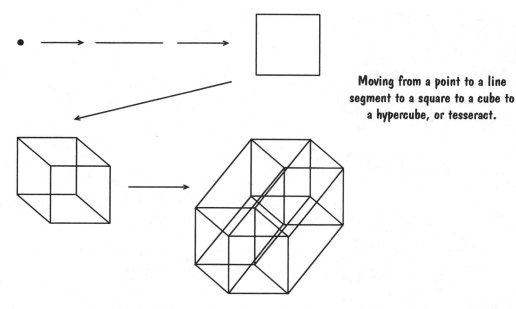

Moving from a point to a line segment to a square to a cube to a hypercube, or tesseract.

A hypercube looks mind-boggling in a two-dimensional drawing on paper, but the fancy graphics of modern computers have allowed mathematicians to create fascinating images on a screen that make it possible to visualize and understand objects, such as hypercubes and hyperspheres, in higher and higher dimensions!

A computer-generated image showing torus-shaped "slices" of a four-dimensional hypersphere.

FROM COMICS TO COSMIC MATH

Mathematician Tom Banchoff as a ten-year-old student on his way to Chicago to appear on a radio quiz show.

As a youth reading Marvel comic books, Thomas Banchoff became fascinated with the idea of objects in the fourth, fifth, or sixth dimension. Now, as a mathematician at Brown University, he is a leader in the study of the geometry of higher dimensions.

Banchoff creates computer graphics that let us visualize objects in the fourth dimension and beyond. His images show how the concept of dimension has significance in mathematics and in the practical world beyond. When we realize that a dimension can represent time, temperature, weight, energy, or other variables, we see that higher dimensions are useful in physics, geology, medicine, and modern art.

Imagine trying to picture what happens in an ecosystem, for example, where rainfall, water temperature, oxygen content, silt depth, and other factors may affect a population of fish living in a lake. We could measure each of the factors separately, then create two-dimensional graphs showing what the population is at different temperatures or different rainfall amounts. If we wanted to show how the population varies with rainfall and temperature at the same time, we would need a three-dimensional graph. To add another variable, we would need a four-dimensional graph!

Finding ways to visualize such complicated systems to try to understand what is going on means learning to think in higher dimensions, just as we can look at an ordinary photograph or study the visual clues in a two-dimensional painting and imagine the three-dimensional shapes those flat pictures represent.

Triangle Tribulations

You are wandering around in the fourth dimension, going in and out of weird holes in the walls, when suddenly a phone rings.

Puzzled, you find the receiver and answer, "Hello."

"This is Digit Three, your old friend from Pi Land."

"Fantastic! Can you help us?" you ask. "We seem to be stuck in the fourth dimension, and we have no idea how to get back into regular space. Will we ever see the stars again? Will we ever return to Earth?"

"That crazy Eight is up to some nasty tricks again," says Three. "When I heard that Eight had sent you guys to the Cubic Grid Galaxy, I knew that you would have a knotty problem and would need my help to get you out."

"How *do* we get out of here? We need to be back in three-dimensional space!"

"Check each corner of your cubic space capsule. In one of the corners you will find a pile of thirty-six cubes about the size of children's building blocks. Arrange the blocks into a perfect triangle. Good luck!"

You hear a click and realize that Three has hung up, so you, Bill, and Anita go and find the thirty-six blocks. How can you arrange them in a perfect triangle?

[Answer follows.]

TRY it

Arrange thirty-six cubes or square tiles into a triangular pattern. The steps below show how to arrange them into a horizontal triangle lying flat on a table or on the floor. If you are using cubes, you may prefer to stack them to form a vertical triangle.

YOU WILL NEED

- Thirty-six sugar cubes or other cubic blocks, or thirty-six squares (about 1 inch or 2.5 centimeters wide) cut from a sheet of paper or cardboard

- flat surface

**WHAT
TO DO**

1. Lay one of the cubes or squares on your surface and place two more below it, like this:

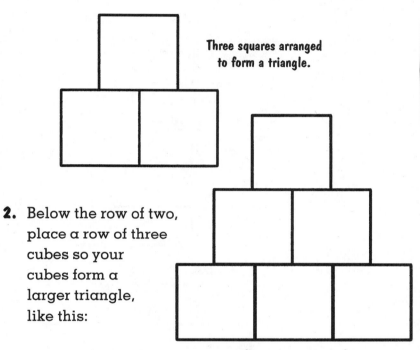

Three squares arranged
to form a triangle.

2. Below the row of two, place a row of three cubes so your cubes form a larger triangle, like this:

Six squares arranged to
form a triangle.

Note that each cube goes beneath a crack between two cubes in the previous row, and the cubes at each end stick out.

3. Make a fourth row using four cubes, and continue adding rows of cubes until you have used up all thirty-six cubes.

[Answer follows.]

Triangular Numbers

Your thirty-six-cube triangle should have eight rows. The first row has just one cube. Each row that follows has one cube more than the previous row. If you count the total number of cubes from the top to a certain row, you get what is known as a triangular number. The first triangular number is 1, followed by 3, 6, 10, 15, 21, 28, 36, and so on.

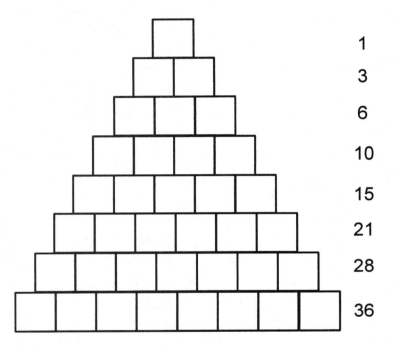

1
3
6
10
15
21
28
36

Counting up the total number of squares required to make up a triangular pattern of a certain number of rows gives a triangular number: 1, 3, 6, 10, 15, 21, 28, and 36.

Triangle Magic

"Now what?" says Anita, staring at the triangle the three of you have formed with the cubes. "We are still stuck in the fourth dimension. This just doesn't add up."

The phone rings again, and you answer.

"I forgot to tell you something," says Three. "You need to number each block."

"No problem. They go from 1 to 36."

"No, no! You have to make everything add up," says Three. "Once they are stacked in a triangle, write '1' on the top cube. Then, on each cube below, write the sum of the cubes above it. Each cube in the second row has a '1' over it, so write '1' on each second-row cube. In the third row, write '1' on the first (left) cube. The center cube has two '1's over it, so write '2.' The third cube has only one '1' over it, so write '1.' Keep on going like that, and you will be amazed by what turns up!"

What is so amazing about those numbers?

[Answer follows.]

TRY it

Label each cube (or square) with the sum of the cubes above it and see what patterns turn up.

YOU WILL NEED
- pencil
- copy of the squares arranged in a triangle on page 88

WHAT TO DO

1. Write "1" on the top square.

2. Write "1" on each of the squares in the second row.

3. Write "1," "2," and "1," in that order, on the cubes in the third row.

4. Number each square in the fourth row with the sum of the squares above it. You should get "1," "3," "3," "1," in that order.

5. Continue numbering the rows in this way until you have numbered all the squares.

6. When you are finished, look for number patterns along rows and diagonals. Try adding the numbers along each row to see what you get.

[Answers follow.]

Pascal's Patterns

The numbered triangle is commonly known as **Pascal's triangle,** named for Blaise Pascal, a French philosopher and mathematician from the seventeenth century. Pascal studied this numbered triangle extensively, but he was not the first to identify it. The Persian poet and mathematician Omar Khayyám (1048–1122) described it in his writings. It also appears in a fourteenth-century Chinese manuscript.

Pascal's triangle is full of interesting number patterns. If you add up the numbers in each row, you get successive powers of 2. For example:

$$\text{Row 1: } 1 = 2^0$$
$$\text{Row 2: } 1 + 1 = 2 = 2^1$$
$$\text{Row 3: } 1 + 2 + 1 = 4 = 2^2$$

The triangle is also full of geometric patterns. If you shade all the squares numbered with a multiple of 5, for example, you get a pattern of upside-down triangles.

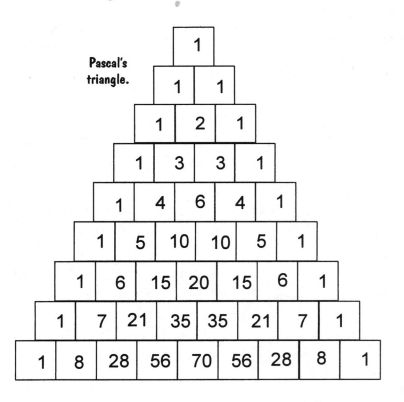

Pascal's triangle.

Look for patterns in Pascal's triangle.

- several copies of Pascal's triangle, page 90
- pencil
- colored pencil (optional)
- calculator (optional)

1. Look for number sequences along the triangle's diagonals.

   The sequence along the first diagonal is
   1, 1, 1, 1, 1, . . .

   The sequence along the second diagonal is
   1, 2, 3, 4, 5, . . .

   Write down the third diagonal sequence. Do you see a pattern?

2. Using a regular or colored pencil, shade all the squares numbered with a multiple of 5. What kind of pattern do you get?

3. Shade all the multiples of 2. How is this pattern different from the pattern in step 2?

4. Try shading multiples of 3, 4, 6, 7, or other numbers, and see what patterns turn up. A calculator may be helpful for dividing very large numbers to see which should be shaded.

5. On any of the shaded triangles, use a different color to shade all the ones, and a third color to shade all the squares you have not yet shaded. What sort of pattern do you see?

[Answers on pp. 107, 108.]

Pascal's Fractals

One of the simplest geometric patterns in Pascal's triangle turns out to be an example of one of the most important geometric shapes in modern mathematics: a **fractal.** In a fractal, each part is made up of scaled-down versions of the whole shape.

When you shade the even numbers (multiples of 2) in Pascal's triangle, the resulting design resembles a special type of fractal called a Sierpinski triangle. This fractal consists of triangles within triangles in a pattern such that smaller triangles contain the same pattern as the larger triangles.

Draw a Sierpinski triangle.

YOU WILL NEED
- pencil and paper
- ruler
- protractor

WHAT TO DO

1. Using your ruler, draw a horizontal line across the page, about 2 inches from the bottom.

2. Use your protractor to draw a 60-degree angle from each end of your horizontal line. Extend the angle rays to form an equilateral triangle.

3. Using your ruler, find and mark the midpoint of each side of the triangle.

4. Connect the three midpoints to form a new set of triangles. Shade the center (upside-down) triangle.

5. For each of the three unshaded triangles, mark the midpoint of each side.

6. Repeat steps 4 and 5 until your triangles get too small to divide.

7. Compare your result with the pattern you got from shading the even numbers in Pascal's triangle.

First stage in creating a Sierpinkski triangle.

[Answer on p. 109.]

THE MAN BEHIND THE TRIANGLE

Blaise Pascal was born in France in 1623. When he was only three years old, his mother died, leaving Blaise and his three sisters with their father, Étienne Pascal. Étienne taught his children at home rather then sending them to school, because he believed that children should not be pushed to study a subject until they could master it easily. He also thought that children's natural curiosity, not a stern teacher, should determine what they are taught. He decided that his children should not study mathematics until age sixteen or so, and he removed all math texts from the house.

Blaise Pascal.

Like a child who is never allowed to watch TV, Blaise became especially curious about the banned subject, mathematics. At age twelve, he started to work on geometry all by himself. Without the aid of a teacher or text, he figured out that the sum of three angles in any triangle is the same as the sum of two right angles (180 degrees). His father was so impressed that he allowed Blaise to study Euclid.

Blaise's sister Jacqueline was also exceptionally talented. She had such a flair for writing poetry that the queen often invited her to the palace, and she was the first girl ever to win a local poetry competition.

Their father, Étienne, was an important government official. As part of France's new ambitious, intellectual nobility, he was acquainted with French mathematicians and other prominent thinkers of the time. When Blaise was fourteen years old, Étienne began bringing him to meetings with Descartes, Fermat, Mersenne, and other prominent mathematicians. By age sixteen, Blaise had been the first to prove some new geometry theorems, which he presented at one of these meetings.

Shortly thereafter, Étienne got a job as a tax collector. To help him out, Blaise invented the first digital calculator.

Pascal's mathematical work greatly influenced leading philosophers and scientists, including René Descartes and Isaac Newton. Pascal's work on the arithmetical triangle (now called Pascal's triangle) led to other important discoveries in mathematics.

Back to Home Base

"**O**NE!" a loud voice blares from your radio. "ONE!" it repeats. "TWO! THREE! FIVE!" the voice booms. Then it stops.

"It repeated '1' and it skipped '4,' just like the Fibonacci sequence," says Anita.

"It sounds like the countdown that brought me into space," you say. "Only this time the count went up instead of down."

"Hey, if the Fibonacci series brought you into space, maybe it also can bring us back to Earth somehow," says Bill.

"But the voice stopped counting," you say. "What if we are stuck here?"

Meanwhile, Anita is studying the numbers on the cubes that form Pascal's triangle. "I bet the Fibonacci sequence is somewhere in Pascal's triangle," she says. "Every number pattern in the universe seems to show up in Pascal's triangle. If we could only find it, we might get somewhere."

The three of you start searching the numbered cubes for Fibonacci numbers, but they don't seem to line up together anywhere in Pascal's triangle. Can you find the Fibonacci sequence by adding or multiplying rows of numbers?

[Answer follows.]

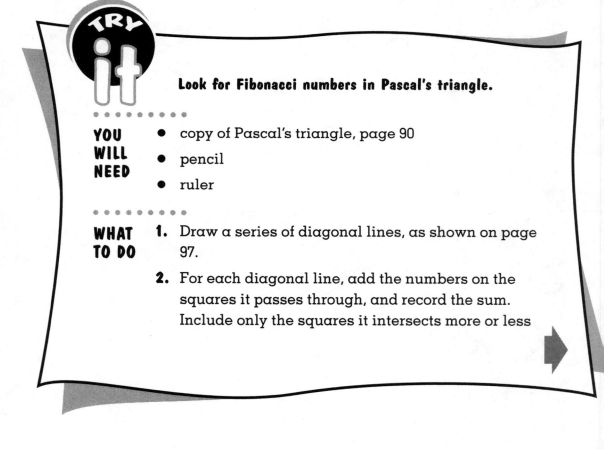

Look for Fibonacci numbers in Pascal's triangle.

YOU WILL NEED
- copy of Pascal's triangle, page 90
- pencil
- ruler

WHAT TO DO

1. Draw a series of diagonal lines, as shown on page 97.

2. For each diagonal line, add the numbers on the squares it passes through, and record the sum. Include only the squares it intersects more or less down the middle. For example, the first line passes only through 1. So does the second line. The third line passes through two 1's, so it has a total of 2. The fourth line passes through 2 and 1, for a total of 3. Do you recognize the numbers?

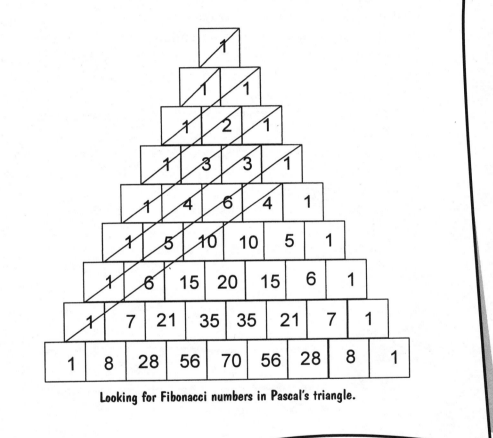

Looking for Fibonacci numbers in Pascal's triangle.

[Answer on page p. 109.]

A Familiar Place

"Awesome!" says Bill as you show him and Anita the Fibonacci sequence you found in Pascal's triangle. Just as you come to the line that adds up to 8, the voice from your radio returns.

"EIGHT!" it blares. An octagon appears on the screen, and the loud motor roars as you feel the spacecraft taking off. Soon the screen is filled with three-dimensional shapes: cubes, tetrahedrons, octahedrons, icosahedrons, and a buckyball. You click on the buckyball, and it grows into a bright, multicolored soccer ball. Admiring its glistening surface of pentagons and hexagons, you click on one of the hexagons. Suddenly the screen fills up with a checkerboard pattern.

The loud motor sounds return, and you feel your stomach rising. Then suddenly it's quiet.

You stand up, walk over to the window, and recognize Checkerboard City.

"It's the Planet of the Shapes! We're back!" you exclaim.

You exit the spacecraft with Anita and Bill, and start taking steps in random directions.

"I'm getting tired, and it seems like we could go forever, walking from square to square," says Anita.

Can you get to the edge of Checkerboard City by moving randomly?

[Answer follows.]

TRY it

Take a random walk on a checkerboard to see if you can get to the edge.

YOU WILL NEED

- checkerboard
- die (You can use a regular six-sided die, but a tetrahedral die is even better, because you only need four sides.)
- checker pieces (or coins or other markers)

**WHAT
TO DO**

1. Find the four center squares on your checkerboard and place a checker piece on one of those squares.

2. Roll the die and take a "step" by placing a second checker piece on the appropriate square: if you roll a 1, place it on the square above; if you roll a 2, place it on the square to the right; 3, on the square below; 4, on the square to the left. If you roll a 5 or a 6, ignore it and roll again.

3. Keep on rolling and placing a checker piece on the appropriate square.

4. How many rolls does it take you to reach the edge of the checkerboard?

5. What kind of pattern do your checker pieces form?

6. Now take a "self-avoiding" random walk (see pages 104–105). Place a checker piece on one of the four center squares, roll the die, and place a second checker piece on the appropriate square.

7. Roll again and place a checker piece on the appropriate square bordering the square you just covered. You may not retrace your "steps," so if the square is already occupied, ignore that roll, and roll again.

8. See if you can reach the edge of the checkerboard before you run out of pieces or get trapped. You will be trapped and unable to move if you end up on a square surrounded by four squares that are already covered.

9. Which gets you to the edge of the checkerboard first, the regular random walk (steps 2–3), or the self-avoiding random walk (steps 6–7)?

[Answers on p. 109.]

Puzzling Pathways

When you, Anita, and Bill reach the edge of Checkerboard City, you find three bicycles and three parallel bike paths. The paths are marked by a sign.

All of the wheels have about the same size diameter, but one bike has square wheels, another has hexagonal wheels, and the third has octagonal wheels.

All of the bike paths are bumpy, but one path has long, tall bumps; one has medium-size bumps; and one has short, relatively flat bumps.

Anita picks up the square-wheeled bike, Bill takes the hexagonal-wheeled bike, and you grab the octagonal-wheeled bike.

Which path should Anita take? What about Bill? Which path will give you the smoothest ride on your octagonal wheels?

(Hint: See "Different Roads for Different Wheels" on page 51.)

[Answers on p. 109.]

Match each wheel with its bike path.

Parting Ways

At the end of the three bike paths, you come to two signs. One sign says "Spaceship Earth" and points to a giant-size soccer ball. It's even larger than the space capsule that you have been riding in.

"That's it!" says Anita, pointing to Spaceship Earth. "That's the taxi that brought us here. It goes back and forth between here and Earth, kind of like a ferryboat. It will take us home!"

You begin to feel a bit homesick and excited, as Bill wanders over to check out the other sign.

"Wow!" he exclaims. "This sign says 'Buckyball Field!'" Then you realize that the sign is pointing to a grassy field where two teams of kids are playing soccer. One team has black shirts, and the other has white shirts, like the ones that Anita and Bill are wearing.

"I think our team needs us," says Bill, just as the black team scores a goal. "Want to join us?" he asks you.

Feeling too tired to play soccer or even to watch the game, you gaze over at Spaceship Earth.

"If you would rather go home, I'm sure that Spaceship Earth will take you," says Anita. "It's a lot like your space capsule. Check it out inside."

"Are you sure you don't want to play just a little bit?" asks Bill.

You can't wait to get home, though, so you bid a fond farewell to your two new friends and head over to Spaceship Earth.

Planet Earth

"THIRTEEN!" blasts a voice from Spaceship Earth. Inside, it looks a lot like the space capsule you have been riding in, only bigger.

"TWENTY-ONE!" it says. You know what the next number will be, of course.

"THIRTY-FOUR!" You start to realize that the giant soccer ball is sailing through space! Looking out the window, you suddenly recognize Earth. You get closer and closer, and a loud motor sounds.

"FIFTY-FIVE!" Suddenly all is peaceful.

You find yourself lying on your bed, looking up at the ceiling. You sit up and suddenly find that your room is no longer a space capsule. It's no longer a mess, either! All your stuff is neatly put away!

You gaze around and look at the walls, the floor, and the ceiling, and remember when they had holes that brought you into the fourth dimension. You think of the tiling pattern on your bathroom floor and realize that its pattern of octagons and squares is like Octagon Square on the Planet of the Shapes. You pick up your old soccer ball and start counting the number of pentagons on its surface.

Through the doorway you begin to sense the delicious smell of apple pie. You think of apples and wonder how many seeds are in an apple. You remember the digits of pi and wonder when you will ever see them again.

Your brain is buzzing with questions. Will you ever get to go back into space? What's the difference between "outer" space and physical space and mathematical space?

There is a knock at your door. "Come in," you say, wondering if the Digits may be visiting, or if Anita and Bill are returning.

Your mother opens the door, and you realize you are back in mundane, earthly reality.

"Great job getting your room in order," she says. "Come and join us for a pie feast!" (or did she say "pi feast"?).

Answers......

Trek 1

Page 4.   The twelfth Fibonacci number is 144. The sixteenth is 987.

Page 4.   The missing numbers are: 76; 96; 44; and 25.

The first set of numbers is an example of a Lucas sequence that begins with 1 and 3, then 1 + 3 = 4, 3 + 4 = 7, 4 + 7 = 11, 7 + 11 = 18, and so on. In the second sequence, the numbers double again and again. In the third, you start with 1, add 2 to get 3, then add 3 to the answer to get 6, then add 4 to the new answer to get 10, and so on. The fourth sequence consists of consecutive perfect squares: $1 \times 1 = 1$, $2 \times 2 = 4$, $3 \times 3 = 9$, and so on.

Page 6.   Some common exceptions are poppy flowers and dogwood flowers, both of which have four petals. Lilies often have six petals.

Page 10.   1. X is $1\frac{1}{8}$ in. (2.8 cm.), and Y is $1\frac{7}{8}$ in. (4.8 cm.).

2. Y/X = 1.666 inches.

3. LM is $1\frac{1}{8}$ in. (2.8 cm.), and LN is $1\frac{3}{4}$ in. (4.375 cm.)

4. LN/LM = 1.555 inches.

Your measurements may be slightly different, but you should come close to the golden ratio, 1.61803 . . .

Trek 2

Page 16.   Squares and triangles fit together in two different ways to form a tiling.

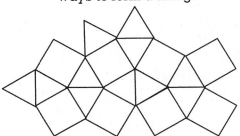
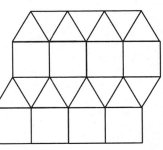

Triangles and hexagons also fit together in two different ways.

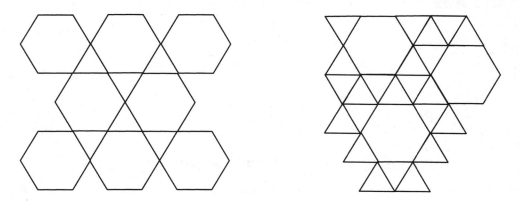

There is just one way to combine triangles, squares, and hexagons.

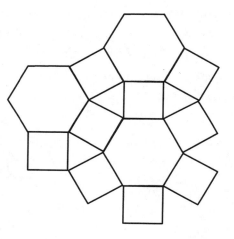

Trek 3

Page 28.   The relationship is F + V = E − 2.

If F = 8 and V = 12, then F+V = 20, so E = 22. That means a polyhedron with 8 faces and 12 vertices has 22 edges!

Page 30.   A soccer ball has 32 faces (20 hexagons and 12 pentagons), so F = 32.

A soccer ball is a truncated icosahedron, so its 12 pentagons come from "slicing off" the 12 vertices of an icosahedron. Therefore, a truncated icosahedron has 12 × 5 = 60 vertices.

F + V = E − 2. Therefore, 32 + 60 = V − 2, so 90 = V − 2, so V = 90.

A soccer ball has 90 vertices.

Trek 5

Page 41. The sum of the angles of a triangle on a sphere is greater than 180 degrees.

The sum of the angles of a four-sided figure on a sphere is greater than 360 degrees. The baseball diamond is a square shape, with all four angles the same size. On a sphere, each angle of a square is greater than 90 degrees. The larger the diamond, the larger the angles on any given sphere.

Page 42. Great Soccer Circles: Yes. Pentagons and hexagons happen to fit together so their edges all meet on great arcs on a sphere. (Because these shapes are rounded on a sphere, their angles are larger than the angles of regular pentagons and hexagons that are flat.)

Page 42. Minipuzzler: The simplest answer is that the pilot started at the North Pole. It is also possible, however, that the pilot started somewhere on a great circle that is 116 kilometers from the South Pole. After flying south 100 kilometers, then east 100 kilometers, she would have completed a circle around the South Pole. Then, when she goes north 100 kilometers, she ends up right back where she started.

Trek 13

Page 59. 1. Length of side of smaller hexagon: $1\frac{1}{16}$ in.

2. Perimeter of smaller hexagon: $1\frac{1}{16} \times 6 = 6.375$ inches

3. Length of side of larger hexagon: $1\frac{1}{4}$ in.

4. Perimeter of larger hexagon: $1\frac{1}{4} \times 6 = 7.5$ inches

5. Estimated circumference of circle: $(6.375 + 7.5) \div 2 = 6.9375$ inches

6. Diameter of circle: $2\frac{1}{8}$ or 2.125 inches

7. Estimated pi: $6.9375 \div 2.125 = 3.2647$

Your measurements may be slightly different, but you should still get a reasonable approximation of the value of pi.

Trek 21

Page 72. Walking on a grid: In a regular (not self-avoiding) random walk your path is darkest around the starting point because the close-in vertices are the ones you end up visiting most frequently. It looks sort of like a road map, where roads and other landmarks are most dense in a city, and fan out around the city's edges.

Page 73. In a self-avoiding random walk your route may form a similar pattern, but you could get trapped at a point where the only possible move is to a place where you have already been.

Trek 34

Page 81. When sides A and B come together, X wins: The bottom row is beside the top row, as shown in the dotted squares at the top of the diagram to the right; also, the top row is next to the bottom row, as shown in the dotted squares at the bottom of the diagram. This creates a diagonal row of three X's.

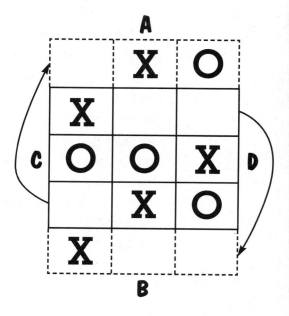

Bringing sides C and D together also produces a diagonal row of three X's, as shown below.

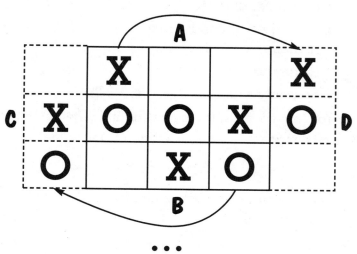

Trek 55

Page 91.

1. The third diagonal in Pascal's triangle is 1, 3, 6, 10, 15, 21 . . . , which forms the following pattern: The second number is the first number plus 2. The third number is the second number plus 3. The fourth number is the third number plus 4, and so on.

2. Shading multiples of 5 in Pascal's triangle produces a pattern of triangles in which each shaded triangle is composed of ten numbers.

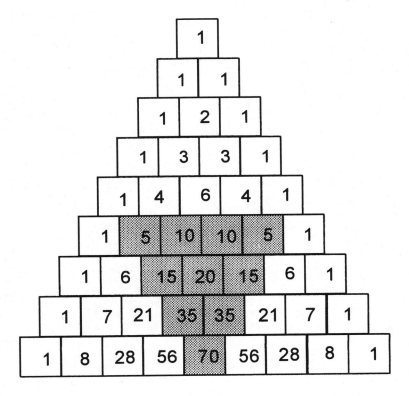

Pascal's triangle with multiples of 5 shaded in.

3. Shading multiples of 2 produces triangles of various sizes, which form the special pattern described on page 92 and pictured on page 109.

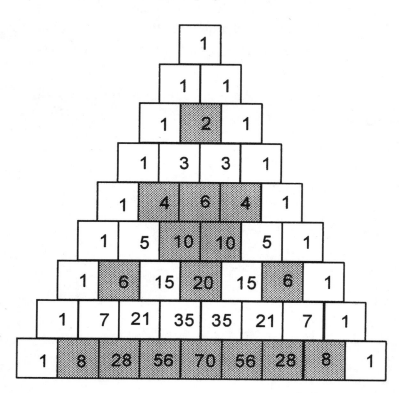

Pascal's triangle with
multiples of 2 shaded in.

4. Multiples of 3, 7, and many other numbers also produce triangle patterns. In each case the triangles are "upside-down," meaning that they point the opposite way from the original Pascal's triangle.

5. Shading the squares that are not multiples of a given number often produces a triangle pattern, with the triangles "right-side up," or pointing the same way as the original Pascal's triangle.

Page 93. A Sierpinski triangle.

Trek 89

Page 97. The fifth line adds up to 5. The next sum is 8, and the Fibonacci series continues with 13, 21, and so on.

Page 99. In the regular checkerboard random walk, you will probably reach the edge of the checkerboard in fewer than fifteen rolls. Your checker pieces will form a ragged pattern that resembles a three-dimensional map of a mountain; the highest piles of checker pieces will be toward the center.

In the self-avoiding random walk, you will probably get to the edge in even fewer steps. You will never reach the edge, however, if you happen to get trapped on a square that is surrounded by checkerboard pieces, which prevent you from moving in any direction.

Page 100. As the number of sides on a polygon increases, it fits shorter and flatter "bumps," or inverted catenaries. (The size of the wheel's radius also affects what size bumps it fits, but in this case, all three bikes have wheels with the same radius.) Anita's square-wheeled bike fits the path with the longest, tallest bumps. Bill's hexagon-wheeled bike fits the path with medium-size bumps, and your octagonal-wheeled bike will get the smoothest ride on the path with the shortest, smallest bumps.

Glossary....................................

buckyball A truncated icosahedron.

catenary The shape formed by a rope, chain, or string hanging loosely from two points. The two points must be at equal height.

circumference The distance around a circle; also called its perimeter.

circumscribed Constructed around the outside of a figure so as to touch as many points of the figure as possible.

cylinder A three-dimensional shape whose cross sections are all circles of the same width. It can be solid like a stick of rock candy or hollow like a tin can.

diameter The distance across a circle, passing through its center and joining two points on its circumference.

Fibonacci sequence A number series first conceived by Leonardo of Pisa, or Fibonacci, in the early thirteenth century. It begins like this: 1, 1, 2, 3, 5, 8, 13, 21, 34, 55 .... To get the next number, you always add the two numbers that came before it.

fractal A type of infinitely repeating shape in which each part is made up of scaled-down versions of the whole structure.

geodesic The shortest curve between two points on a three-dimensional surface.

golden ratio A line segment (C) is divided into "golden section" if its smaller part (A) divided by its larger part (B) equals B divided by C. (A/B = B/C.) If A = 1, then B is the golden ratio. The symbol for the golden ratio is τ. The number τ always equals $\frac{1}{2}(1 + \sqrt{5})$, or about 1.6180.

golden rectangle A rectangle with sides that correspond to the golden ratio.

great circle   The circular edge of a sphere cut exactly in half. Also, the largest circle that can be drawn on the surface of a sphere.

hexagon   A six-sided polygon.

hyperspace   Four-dimensional space.

icosahedron   A polyhedron with 20 faces. A regular icosahedron has triangular faces, each one an equilateral triangle.

inscribed   Drawn within a figure so as to touch as many points of the figure as possible.

irrational number   A number that cannot be written in the form a/b, where a and b are integers. Expressed in decimal notation, an irrational number has an infinite number of digits to the right of the decimal point, and the digits follow no repeating pattern.

Lucas sequence   A number series named after nineteenth-century French number theorist Édouard Lucas, who studied the Fibonacci sequence and similar sequences, such as the Lucas sequence, which begins: 1, 3, 4, 7, 11, 18 . . .

manifold   A certain type of higher-dimensional object in which opposite sides are connected through a higher dimension.

Pascal's triangle   A triangular pattern of numbers in which each number is the sum of the two numbers above it. (See page 90.)

pentagon   A five-sided polygon.

perimeter   The length of the boundary, or outside edge, of a flat figure.

periodic   Repeating. A periodic design has a pattern of one or more repeating parts.

pi   The circumference of a circle divided by its diameter.

plane   An infinitely wide flat surface.

Platonic solid   A polyhedron whose surface is composed of regular polygons.

polygon A flat shape with three or more sides. Generally each side is straight, not curved.

polyhedron A three-dimensional shape whose surface is composed of polygons. (Plural: polyhedra.)

radius The distance from a circle's center to its edge (the diameter divided by 2).

random walk Step-by-step movement from point to point, in which the direction is chosen randomly.

regular polygon A flat shape with three or more sides, in which all sides are of equal length and the sides form angles of equal size. Furthermore, all of the vertices can be connected to form a circle.

self-avoiding random walk A random walk that never goes to the same point more than once.

symmetry Balance and regularity. In a symmetrical design, parts on different sides of a dividing line correspond in shape, size, and relative position.

torus A three-dimensional object shaped like a doughnut.

truncated icosahedron A polyhedron composed of twenty regular hexagons and twelve regular pentagons.

vertex A corner of a shape. In a polygon, a vertex is the point where two sides meet, whereas in a polyhedron, it is where three or more faces or edges meet.

Further Readings......................

Visit the Math Trek web site at http://home.att.net/~mathtrek/ to find additional material and references, amusing puzzles and features, and links to web sites on Fibonacci numbers, random walks, four-dimensional geometry, and other topics. Send us e-mail at mathtrek@worldnet.att.net.

General   Hans Magnus Enzensberger. *The Number Devil: A Mathematical Adventure* (New York: Henry Holt, Metropolitan Books, 1997).

Jane Muir. *Of Men and Numbers: The Story of the Great Mathematicians* (Mineola, N.Y.: Dover, 1996).

Ivars Peterson. *The Mathematical Tourist: New and Updated Snapshots of Modern Mathematics* (New York: W. H. Freeman, 1998).

Ivars Peterson and Nancy Henderson. *Math Trek: Adventures in the MathZone* (New York: John Wiley & Sons, 2000).

Michael Serra. *Discovering Geometry: An Inductive Approach*, 2nd ed. (Berkeley, Calif.: Key Curriculum Press, 1997).

David Wells. *The Penguin Dictionary of Curious and Interesting Numbers*, rev. ed. (New York: Penguin, 1997).

Trek 1   Rob Eastaway and Jeremy Wyndham. *"Why Can't I Find a Four-Leafed Clover?"* In *Why Do Buses Come in Threes? The Hidden Mathematics of Everyday Life* (New York: John Wiley & Sons, 1998).

Martin Gardner. "Fibonacci and Lucas numbers." In *Mathematical Circus* (Washington, D.C.: Mathematical Association of America, 1992).

Martin Gardner. "Phi: The Golden Ratio." In *The 2nd Scientific American Book of Mathematical Puzzles and Diversions* (New York: Simon & Schuster, 1961).

Ivars Peterson. "Nature's Numbers." *Muse 3* (November 1999): 25.

Ian Stewart. *Nature's Numbers: The Unreal Reality of Mathematics* (New York: HarperCollins, Basic Books, 1995).

Trek 2   Martin Gardner. "Penrose Tiling." In *Penrose Tiles to Trapdoor Ciphers ... and the Return of Dr. Matrix* (Washington, D.C.: Mathematical Association of America, 1997).

Martin Gardner. "Tiling with Convex Polygons." In *Time Travel and Other Mathematical Bewilderments* (New York: W. H. Freeman, 1988).

Doris Schattschneider. *Visions of Symmetry. Notebooks, Periodic Drawings, and Related Works of M. C. Escher* (New York: W. H. Freeman, 1990).

Trek 3   J. Baldwin. *BuckyWorks: Buckminster Fuller's Ideas for Today* (New York: John Wiley & Sons, 1996).

Martin Gardner. "The Five Platonic Solids." In *The Unexpected Hanging: And Other Mathematical Diversions* (Chicago: University of Chicago Press, 1991).

Trek 5   D. Burger. *Sphereland: A Fantasy about Curved Spaces and an Expanding Universe,* translated by C. J. Rheiboldt (New York: Barnes & Noble Books, 1965).

István Lénárt. *Non-Euclidean Adventures on the Lénárt Sphere: Investigations in Planar and Spherical Geometry* (Berkeley, Calif.: Key Curriculum Press, 1996).

Trek 8   Martin Gardner. "Curves of Constant Width." In *The Unexpected Hanging: And Other Mathematical Diversions* (Chicago: University of Chicago Press, 1991).

Ivars Peterson. "Covering Up." *Muse 3* (July/August 1999): 36.

Ivars Peterson. "Square Wheel." *Muse 3* (February 1999): 29.

Stan Wagon. "The Ultimate Flat Tire." *Math Horizons* (February 1999): 14–17.

Trek 13   Petr Beckmann. *A History of π (Pi)* (New York: St. Martin's Press, 1971).

David Blatner. *The Joy of π* (New York: Walker and Company, 1997).

Martin Gardner. "The Transcendental Number Pi." In *Martin Gardner's New Mathematical Diversions from Scientific American* (New York: Simon & Schuster, 1966).

Trek 21   Martin Gardner. "Random Walks on the Plane and in Space." In *Mathematical Circus* (Washington, D.C.: Mathematical Association of America, 1992).

Ivars Peterson. *The Jungles of Randomness: A Mathematical Safari* (New York: John Wiley & Sons, 1998).

Trek 34   Edward A. Abbott. *Flatland: A Romance of Many Dimensions* (Princeton, N.J.: Princeton University Press, 1991).

Thomas F. Banchoff. *Beyond the Third Dimension: Geometry, Computer Graphics, and Higher Dimensions* (New York: Scientific American Library, 1990).

Trek 55   Martin Gardner. "Pascal's Triangle." In *Mathematical Carnival* (Washington, D.C.: Mathematical Association of America, 1988).

Martin Gardner. "Mandelbrot's Fractals." In *Penrose Tiles to Trapdoor Ciphers . . . and the Return of Dr. Matrix* (Washington, D. C.: Mathematical Association of America, 1997).

Ian Stewart. "Pascal's Fractals." In *Game, Set, and Math: Enigmas and Conundrums* (Oxford, Eng.: Basil Blackwell, 1989).

Index..